CONTENTS

SHOW JUMPING MADE EASY

SHOW JUMPING MADE EASY
THE WAY TO SUCCESSFUL SHOW JUMPING

CLARISSA BUSCH

Copyright of original edition © 1999 by Cadmos Verlag
Copyright of this edition © 2003 by Cadmos Verlag
Translated by Konstanze Allsopp
Layout: Ravenstein Brain Pool
Title Photo: Werner Ernst
Print: Westermann Druck Zwickau GmbH
Printed in Germany.
ISBN 3-86127-907-X

With sufficient balance, even small fences can be jumped bareback.
Photo: S. Stuewer

INTRODUCTION

BASIC RIDER REQUIREMENTS

Before any rider can start jumping fences, he/she must have achieved a balanced and relaxed seat. Clinging onto the reins because you have insufficient balance in the saddle will under most circumstances impair your control of the horse. The ability to keep a balanced position during the jump is a funda-

mental requirement for jumping. Riders who want to start learning to jump should preferably have learned to hack out securely and independently. In my opinion, hacking out is the ideal preparation to teach the rider how to manage his horse and to anticipate its reaction to unfamiliar things. The rider will have acquired a secure seat, should the horse suddenly shy and jump to one side. Being able to stay in the saddle in such a situation is the pre-requisite for jumping.

The rider is wearing the correct outfit, with a splinter-proof hat with a three-point harness, riding boots and gloves. Photo: A. Busch

EQUIPMENT

For safety reasons a rider should always wear an approved riding helmet. This is particularly important when jumping. It is essential in this context that the hat with its chin strap is fitted correctly, in order to prevent it from falling off or slipping during a fall. In my opinion, a jockey's crash helmet with a three-point harness is better suited for this purpose, especially for young riders, and of course they are obligatory at any competition. With a good-looking hat silk, these hats look elegant and offer a high degree of protection. All hats should comply with the PAS015 and BSEN1384 standards. A back-protector (as required in eventing) is also a sensible addition to the rider's outfit. Correct footwear, preferably long riding or jodhpur boots should be worn as a matter of course. Wearing extra protection for jumping has got nothing to do with fear or bad riding. Even the most expe-

rienced riders will fall off occasionally, and there is no point in injuring oneself needlessly and risking loss of confidence in the future.

Apart from the rider's clothes, a short jumping stick or spurs will be necessary, depending on the predisposition of the horse. The motto here is to be equipped for an emergency (a refusal), but to use as few aids as possible in order to prevent the horse from becoming desensitised.

THE RIGHT HORSE

If the rider himself is inexperienced, he should learn to jump on an experienced horse which jumps willingly. The danger of turning a horse "sour" so that it keeps on refusing is very real and the chances of retraining a horse that persistently refuses are small. If this happens, the horse will no longer be suitable for show jumping and the rider, too, will become insecure as he will constantly fear that his horse will stop. As his aids will still be inadequate or incorrect, the inexperienced rider will make the horse feel insecure, and only a very experienced horse can compensate for this deficit. It also makes sense for a good show jumping rider to school an experienced horse, from time to time, as even the experienced horse could otherwise lose its confidence under an inexperienced rider, which will lead to refusals, even if the horse has always co-operated in the past.

Sometimes, riding pupils tell me: "My horse never stops." I always warn them not to become complacent and depend too much on their horse's talent, and also not to overdo things,

An inexperienced rider will gain a lot of confidence and a feeling of security on an older, experienced horse. Photo: C. Busch

because once a horse is forced to jump beyond its capabilities, or injures itself at a fence, even a horse which has always jumped will soon start refusing constantly as a matter of course. Almost all horses which tend to refuse started off in this way. Usually a young horse will be very courageous over fences, but incorrect aids will make it feel insecure very quickly.

This, however, should not stop you from learning to jump. I just want to make it absolutely clear that, compared to dressage, it is very easy to spoil a horse during jumping, which will have lasting effects. Riders should learn to handle the issue of jumping in a responsible manner and ask for less rather than too much.

THE JUMPING SEAT

To ride in the jumping seat, which is practised in the first lessons, the rider needs to shorten his stirrups by two to

three holes from the dressage length. The exact length of the stirrup leather will depend on each rider's personal feeling of comfort. Some riders prefer to ride with very long stirrups, others choose extremely short stirrups. It is important that the rider is able to take

In the beginning, jumps can be built with simple materials. Photo: S. Stuewer

To start off with, the jumping - or forward - seat should be practised at the trot. The rider raises his buttocks off the saddle very slightly and thereby shifts his weight into the stirrups. The most common fault is rising too high in the saddle and shifting the weight too far forward onto the horse's shoulders. The rider must prevent this at all costs. He should always maintain his weight over the centre of balance of the horse. At the moment of take-off, the horse needs to have complete freedom of its shoulders, in order to be able to gain sufficient height. In order to teach riders to balance their weight centrally above the horse, I let them practise maintaining balance with bent knees and hips, standing on the ground. They have to learn to balance their upper body with bent knee and hip joints without tipping forward. This makes the art of maintaining one's balance on horseback much easier to comprehend. Another useful exercise is riding in the forward position without stirrups.

The correct balance of the rider, demonstrated on the ground. Photo: C. Busch

the weight off the saddle and to lift his buttocks 10 to 20 centimetres from the saddle, while maintaining the correct leg position. In order to check the stirrup length, I ask the riders to adopt the jumping position at a halt and make sure that their legs remain close to their horse's sides in the correct position. If the rider is able to raise himself slightly out of the saddle, the stirrup length is correct. If possible, you should always use a jumping or eventing saddle, or at least a general purpose saddle. The knee supports, fitted specifically for jumping, ensure that the rider's legs remain more firmly in the correct position and improve the rider's seat during the jump. Dressage saddles are not suitable for show jumping. The saddle flaps of jumping saddles are shorter and broader to accommodate the more acute angle of the rider's knees.

To begin with, the rider should support his weight by placing his hands on the horse's neck, as this will stop him giving in to the temptation of hanging onto the reins. In special cases, a neck strap can be used for the rider to hold onto. The reins are held at the same time. The more balanced the rider becomes, the less he will have to resort to holding on for support.

An even, close contact with both legs is imperative during jumping. The entire lower leg, including foot and heel, must lie against the horse's side in a steady, fixed position. The rider's knee should be placed against the horse, but without the use of excessive for-

The rider's lower leg maintains its correct position below the centre of balance even during the actual jump.
Photo: Schmelzer

ce, as this would cause the lower leg to lose its firm contact and position. Depending on the anatomy of your horse, the correct position of the lower leg will be more or less easy to maintain. It is however essential that you achieve this position in order to gain a secure jumping seat and to prevent the horse from running out at the fence, or refusing. The knees and ankles have to function like a spring in order to compensate for the swing of the horse over the fence. The rider's heels have to flex as far down as possible, with the stirrups in the correct position on the balls of the feet. A stiff ankle (even with a heel pressed well down) must be avoided at all costs.

Once the rider is able to maintain a balanced seat at the trot, this needs to be practised at the canter. It is imperative that the forward seat is executed correctly, in order to relieve the horse's back, and it is the fundamental prerequisite for the rider to follow the horse correctly over the jump. The forward seat is used in between the individual fences and in particular over a fence itself. During the approach to a fence, however, the rider should sit deeper in the saddle. As the rider keeps his upper body in a forward position during the approach, contrary to the dressage seat, this is also a form of the forward seat.

It is important that the rider is able to influence the horse with his aids whilst sitting in the forward position. The forward-driving as well as restraining aids need to be applied to relax the horse and ensure it responds to the rider in the same way as this is achieved with the dressage seat. It is imperative for the show jumping rider to practise this in his daily schooling sessions.

The rider relieves the horse's back and supports her hands on the horse's neck at the same time.

THE FIRST JUMPS

CAVALETTIS AND TROTTING-POLES

Once the rider has practised the jumping seat on the flat, he can start work over trotting-poles. To begin with, riding over trotting poles is used to improve the balance of the rider. For this purpose, three or four poles or cavalettis in their lowest position are placed in a row covering a distance of approximately 1.2 metres to 1.4 metres. Cavalettis are more suitable, as they cannot be displaced by the horse

should it step on one. If your horse has had little experience with trotting-poles, it is sensible to accustom the horse first by walking over the poles. For this purpose, the poles are placed between 80 and 100 centimetres apart. (All distances are dependent on the size of the horse and its length of stride. Naturally a pony will require shorter distances than a very large horse. The distances quoted here are average figures which can be changed, depending on the horse's requirements.)

Once the horse has been acquainted with poles, the rider trots over these in the forward seat, taking particular care to focus on the correct seat and posture. This exercise is designed for the rider to practise the balanced seat over a fence. Here, as always, the centre of balance should not be shifted too far forward or back, and the rider has to stay in rhythm with the motion of the horse. Riding trotting-poles at the rising trot does not fulfil this purpose. The rider should flex smoothly at the hip without falling onto the horse's back. The hands maintain a light but constant contact with the horse's mouth. The rider's legs swing steadily at the horse's sides, driving the horse forwards evenly.

The rider compensates for the swing of the horse's back through increased flexion of the ankle, knee and hip joints. The rider must not bump down in the saddle. As before, the rider is permitted to support his hands on each side of the horse's neck.

The exercise is ideal for practising the correct jumping seat over fences.

If the horse runs out to one side of the cavaletti, I usually place two poles at a 90 degree angle to and on the approach side of the trotting lane, and move these closer together once the horse has become accustomed to them. Finally, the poles are placed no more than 1.5 metres apart, allowing the horse a narrow passage towards the centre of the trotting lane. This will prevent it from running out, and the rider can concentrate on his seat with no distractions.

Right from the start, the rider should also learn to look straight ahead, in a jumping ring as well as over the fences themselves. This is important, on the one hand to keep track of the correct course, as the rider will need to keep the next obstacle in view as soon as he has jumped the previous one. In addition, looking at the ground will upset the balance of horse and rider over a fence, as the rider's

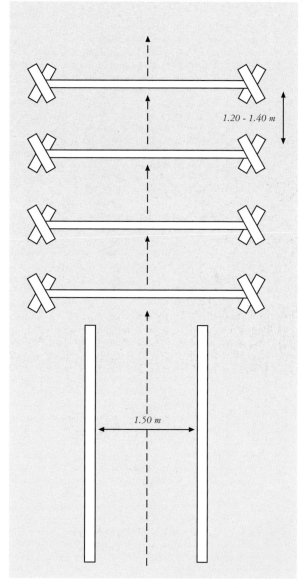

head with its own not inconsiderable weight will in turn pull the rider's weight forward, and the weight will also be distributed unevenly to the side the rider is looking down at. The rider has to learn to feel how his horse jumps.

Riding over trotting poles will also give the rider a feel for the correct approach to the fence. In order to be

The two poles prevent the horse from running out to either side.

1.20 - 1.40 m

1.50 m

Unusual fence variations make for interesting changes during schooling sessions.
Photo: Schmelzer

able to ride "correctly" over trotting poles, he has to encourage the horse to pick up its foreleg at a certain distance from the first pole. Each leg should be placed rhythmically and evenly in the centre between the individual poles. At the trot, the correct distance to the first pole is between 60 and 70 centimetres. Judging this distance determines whether a horse makes a good job of his task and trots over the poles in even strides, or loses his rhythm. This always happens if the horse takes off too far away or too close to the first pole. The rider should take note of when the horse takes the poles spot on, or when it lifts its leg too far away or too near the pole. Often, I change the distances of the trotting-poles for exercise, so that the horse has to take them at an energetic working trot or at other times at a more sedate, almost collected pace. Changing the distances is a good training for the feeling of rhythm of horse and rider.

Jumping quadrilles teaches riders to judge their approach and improve the feeling of being in balance with the horse. Photo: Schmelzer

JUMPING FROM THE TROT

Once the rider is able to ride over the trotting-poles on the ground securely and in balance, I put up another cavaletti in its highest position, or a low cross pole at 40 centimetres approximately 2.2 metres behind the trotting-poles. Initially, this jump should be equipped with wings to stop the horse from running out. As before, the rider will trot over the trotting-poles in the forward seat, remaining in this position when the horse then jumps over the small following fence. At first, he should lean forward a bit earlier, so as not to get left behind during the horse's movement over the fence and thus pull at its mouth. It is not necessary for the rider to raise his buttocks any higher going over a fence as small as this, than over the trotting-poles. The centre of balance should always remain underneath the seat bones.

Most riders have a tendency to stand up over even the smallest fence, as if they were about to jump a high oxer (parallel bar). How far you rise in the saddle is not important, but rather how well you balance your weight over the fence, keeping your lower legs in the correct position enclosing the horse firmly. The rider should always feel his weight on both legs in the stirrups.

THE REIN AIDS DURING THE JUMP

Another very important factor in jumping is the giving of the reins during the moment of suspension over the jump in order to allow the horse optimum freedom of its head during the jump. The horse needs this to maintain its own and the rider's weight in balance over the jump. Keeping the horse's and rider's balance and equilibrium is

the most important thing in show jumping. If a beginner continuously pulls his horse in the mouth because he is constantly left behind, there is a real danger that even the most willing showjumper will start to refuse, in order to evade the punishing treatment over the fence. Therefore, I make sure even when they are jumping low fences, that my riding pupils do not hang onto the reins but instead support their hand well down on the horse's neck and give the reins sufficiently so that these hang in a loop during the jump. The rider's hands should always move along the horse's neck in the direction of the horse's mouth. They should not

The rider's hands move forward on the horse's neck to allow it complete freedom of its head over the fence. Photo: A. Busch

When approaching the fence, the rider maintains sufficient contact with the reins. Over the fence itself she gives the reins and supports both hands on the horse's neck. Photo: A. Busch

The rider learns in play to support her hands as low as possible on the horse's neck. Photo: Schmelzer

however come too close to the horse's ears, as this can disturb the horse during the jump.

In order that the rider does not interfere with the horse over a fence in the forward seat, the elasticity of the his shoulders is of particular importance. He will have to follow the horse's movements flexibly from the shoulder. Later in the course of the training, the rider learns to maintain a light contact with the horse's mouth. Initially, it is better if the reins hang in loops so that the rider learns to follow the horse's movement independently. During the approach towards the fence, however, it is important to maintain contact to prevent the horse from running out. Letting the reins hang loosely over the jump is also important in case the horse does not take off correctly. If this happens, the horse needs an optimum freedom of its head and neck, so it can find its balance sufficiently to get both itself and the rider out of an awkward situation. The rider needs to practise this reaction extensively over small fences, so that this action comes automatically in an emergency. Trotting over the poles, the horse should stretch forwards and downwards as far as possible in order to loosen its back muscles and achieve a higher degree of bascule (rounding and stretching of the back). The reins have to be long enough to allow this and at the same time maintain a flexible connection with the horse's mouth, similar to an elastic band. This connection is maintained up to the point of take-off. Over the jump at the point of suspension, the reins should be slack. In particular, the rider must not pull his hands up over the jump, but keep them low on the horse's neck.

During this stage, it is also useful to introduce a cross fence with one take-off pole (approximately 2.5 metres in front of the fence). It is extremely important to learn the correct forward seat over individual, low fences, as this allows the rider to concentrate entirely on his seat, and he does not have to concentrate on the fences as he would normally have to, jumping a course or a higher fence. The correct seat must become second nature.

Another important feature is the careful taking-up of the reins at the point of landing. The rider must prevent a sudden pull on the reins after the jump at all costs, as this would seriously damage the trust of the horse.

At the moment of landing the rider should straighten his upper body and slowly shorten the reins again, so that he can push the horse forwards into his hands at the first stride after the fence.

LEG AIDS FOR THE TAKE-OFF IMPULSE

The next aid the rider learns is to ask his horse to take off in front of the fence with his lower leg. This aid will be almost unnecessary in the case of a very experienced horse, as it will know exactly when to take off itself. The rider, however, has to get a feel for the right moment in which to press both calves against the horse's side with a short energetic push or a light kick. The horse itself should also be schooled in this manner to achieve a harmonised moment of take-off.

This new aid is again practised over a small fence with a take-off pole on the approach side. The rider trots towards the pole at a rhythmic tempo and uses both legs to drive the horse forwards. This can be done at the rising trot. Shortly before reaching the take-off pole, the rider should adopt the forward seat. When the horse lifts

*The rider gives the horse sufficient impulse with her legs for the take-off.
Photo: C. Busch*

its first leg over the pole, the rider should push with both legs to give a take-off impulse. The aid for the horse to take off not only tells the horse the right moment to take off, but also encourages it to push off energetically with its hindquarters and jump with "bounce", as show jumpers call it. If the horse does not react to the rider's leg aids, it can be useful to employ the voice as an extra aid, by clicking the tongue at the exact moment at which the horse is expected to take off. In extreme cases, the rider taps the horse on the shoulder with the jumping whip to gain the horse's attention. The voice aid can also come from the riding instructor. I often accompany my riding pupils up to the fence in the beginning by saying rhythmically "trot, trot, trot ..." and then "... and jump" or "... and push". The take-off pole determines the point of take-off so far in advance that the rider will soon get a feeling for the correct moment of take-off.

RIDING POLES AT THE CANTER

At the same time as learning how to jump small fences from the trot, the rider also learns to approach a fence at the canter. Approaching a fence at the canter is significantly more difficult than approaching it at the trot, because the horse is only able to jump a fence if it has finished the sequence of the preceding canter stride: it is unable to take off at the canter at any other moment. Jumping a fence is simply taking a larger stride at the canter. Depending on the length of the horse's stride at the

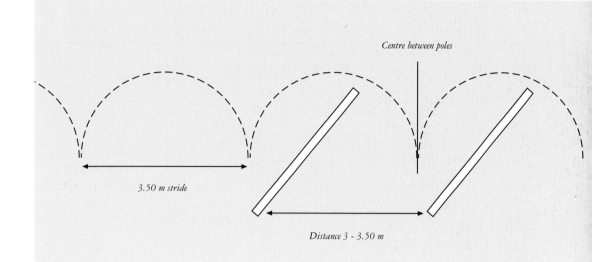

Centre between poles

3.50 m stride

Distance 3 - 3.50 m

The horse can only take off at a canter at the end of a stride of 3 to 3.5 metres.

canter, a horse requires 3.5 to 4.5 metres for each full phase. If the horse is trotting, it can take off with each forward motion of the diagonal pair of legs, in other words every 1 to 1.5 metres. At the canter, this is only possible around every 3.5 metres. It is far more difficult to get this distance right in front of a fence, and therefore, it can happen that the horse takes off too early because it is unable to fit in another stride. Therefore it will sometimes take off earlier or later than the rider expects, making it difficult for him to "stay" with the horse over the jump.

To begin with, the rider learns to canter over poles on the ground. For this purpose, he rides a rhythmic tempo and drives the horse forward to the pole at a steady pace. Try avoiding pulling the horse's head too far over to the leading side of its front legs (canter on the right and canter on the left rein). During jumping the horse should always approach the fence as straight as possible. It should approach the fence between the reins and rider's

legs as if on rails. When riding over poles on the ground the rider simply gives with his hands. It is not necessary to lift oneself out of the saddle.

With growing experience, further poles are laid behind the first one at intervals of approximately 3.5 metres. These are taken at a rhythmic canter. The rider should concentrate on finding and maintaining the correct distances in order to practise judging the take-off.

JUMPING FROM THE TROT WITHOUT A TAKE-OFF POLE

Approaching a fence without a take-off pole at the trot also helps to improve the rider's eye for the correct take-off. The best fence to practise this with is a cross-pole. It automatically guides the horse to the middle of the fence, making the process easier for the rider. If the horse runs out to one side of the

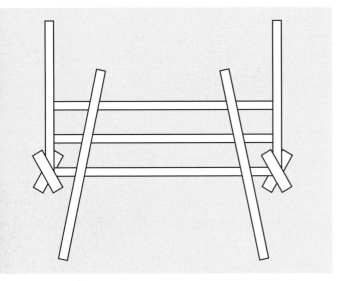

The two poles guide the horse straight over the fence.

The line in the sand acts as a take-off aid and shows the rider the ideal point of take-off. Photo: C. Busch

movement of the horse in case it takes off too early. The horse will take off approximately 1 metre in front of the fence. I often draw an approximate take-off line in the sand with my foot, to make it easier for the rider to follow the horse's movement. In time, he will learn always to "stay" with the horse and ask the horse to take off at the correct moment. Teacher and pupil should allow sufficient time for this, as finding the correct point of take-off and staying with the horse over the jump form the basis for good show jumping.

Jumping without a take-off pole is clearly more difficult. Both horse and rider have to deal with the problem of deciding when to take off without the help of a preceding pole. This exercise is easier when carried out at the trot and the rider will become more secure because of it. There is such a multitude of things to learn over small fences that it is completely unnecessary to start on

fence despite the cross-pole, two poles can be placed on the ground or even on the fence at a ninety degree angle to direct the horse towards the centre of the fence.

The rider should approach the fence in the forward seat, not at a rising trot, in order not to get too far behind the

higher fences in the first weeks and even months. The confidence which the rider learns here will be invaluable later.

If the horse starts to rush fences during jumping, the rider should calmly turn it away from the fence (not, however, exactly in front of the fence but at a distance of around 15 metres before, as the horse would otherwise learn to refuse) and ride it around quietly until it is listening to the rider's aids again. Then approach the fence anew. If the horse still rushes the fence, it is also possible to approach it at a walk and only push it into a trot a few strides away from the fence. The horse is perfectly capable of jumping small fences from a standstill. An inexperienced rider will feel insecure on a horse which rushes its fences and he will be unable to learn the correct aids for the approach.

SMALL FENCES
FROM THE CANTER

Now is the time to start jumping cavalettis or small cross-poles from the canter. Individual fences are approached in the same manner as the above mentioned poles lying on the ground. Initially, I help the rider to find the correct rhythm for the take-off with my voice. Once the rider has jumped this individual fence in a relaxed manner, I add a second small jump or cavaletti behind the first fence at a distance of 3 to 3.5 metres, which creates a low in-out, in order to improve the feeling of rhythm. "In-out" means that the horse jumps the second fence immediately, without an additional stride between the two

obstacles. This especially improves the feeling of rhythm of the rider. He will learn to give with his hands and push with his legs rhythmically.

Jumping in-out fences from the trot increase the feeling of rhythm of the horse and rider at the fence.
Photo: Schmelzer

The rider distinctly sits down in the saddle and straightens her upper body between the fences.
Photo: C. Busch

JUMPING GRIDS

Grids are an ideal tool to teach the rider the feeling of rhythm, balance and correct take-off distance. The best way to tackle grids is to approach the row of fences at a trot with a take-off pole as an aid, as this ensures that the horse arrives at the first fence with correct stride and will be able to jump each following fence without difficulty if the grid has been built correctly. This teaches both horse and rider confidence.

There is a multitude of ways in which to design a grid. For example, an in-out made from cross-poles can follow the take-off pole at a distance of 3 metres followed after 6 metres by another small fence. The distances are dependent on the pace adopted on the approach to the grid. If the rider approaches at a trot, the distances will always be a little shorter than from the canter.

If there is space for one or more strides between the fences, the rider has to learn to sit back down in the saddle and pick up the reins as he did before the first fence. Each fence is thus approached individually. The rider will have to practise to sit down gently in the saddle during the landing phase, to pick up the reins smoothly at the same time and immediately concentrate on the next fence in the row during the first canter stride after landing. Almost all riders later find combinations and related distances the most difficult fences to jump (combinations have one or two strides between the fences, related distances three or four strides). If the rider has practised these right from the start however, combinations will pre-

Jumping correctly paced combinations at an inviting height should form a substantial part of the basic training.
Photo: Stuewer

sent few problems later on and the increase in height will not present a difficulty for the rider, if he has learned to approach the first fence correctly and jump the combination rhythmically. Gridwork particularly trains the eye and the feeling for the correct distance. If jumping grids has become an easy task, the rider can start to approach grids from the canter. Here again, a take-off pole at a distance of 3 metres, or a small in-out, should be built at the start of the grid to ensure that the horse always approaches the following fences at the correct distance. These can then be slowly increased in height

The horse is prepared for higher oxers by jumping a suitable grid in the course of its schooling.
Photo: Schmelzer

and width. Thus the rider learns to jump higher fences from the grid, which gives him the confidence of getting the take-off right. The best way to proceed here, is to increase individual fences slowly up to the take-off of a slightly higher and wider oxer, because the horse gains increasing confidence for the correct distance with every preceding jump. All the rider has to do is count the canter strides, in other words for two strides between the fences (around 10.5 metres) "Land - one - two-take-off", so that he always knows the exact take-off point. Naturally, it is important to raise the height of the jumps slowly. Far more important here is that the rider becomes accustomed to jumping oxers, which many inexperienced riders are afraid of. The grids

should be built and set up in the course of a lesson. After the horse has been warmed up over trotting-poles and smaller fences, the grid is set up fence by fence at a low level to slowly accustom horse and rider to the task. Then the height of the fences is increased slowly. A refusal at this stage, because the rider is expected to jump the entire grid at its maximum height right from the start, should be avoided at all costs, because this leads to negative feelings in the rider regarding combinations. Approaching unaccustomed grids or rows of fences is something the rider learns later on during his training.

JUMPING ON A CIRCLE

Once the rider has learnt to jump individual fences and grids correctly, it is time to start jumping on a circle. I usually put up a simple cross-pole on the circle and divide the riders into two or more groups of no more than three riders per group. These now initially approach the cross-pole on the circle from a trot over a take-off pole. The horse should canter at the landing and recovery stage. In the beginning, the difficulty lies predominantly in the approach on a curved line. The rider needs to bend the horse so it follows the circle line. Both reins have even contact, both rider's legs frame the horse and restrict it in the bend until the horse reaches the fence and the rider gives the aids for the take-off. Under no circumstances should the rider let his horse ride straight lines and simply bend in the corners. In a show jumping course it is often necessary to jump fences at an angle from a bend. It is important that the rider learns to start concentrating on the fence fifteen metres before take-off and to aim at the centre of the fence. He has to maintain the horse on the correct line with his legs, in other words, the inside leg pushes the horse out, if necessary, and the outside leg restricts the horse if it tries to swing out too far.

In principle, it is better to use a circle with a smaller rather than a larger diameter. If the horse is ridden too close to the inside stand, it may drift to the outside during the actual jump and correct the distance. Approaching from the outside to the inside of the fence is more likely to provoke the horse to refuse. On a circle it is always

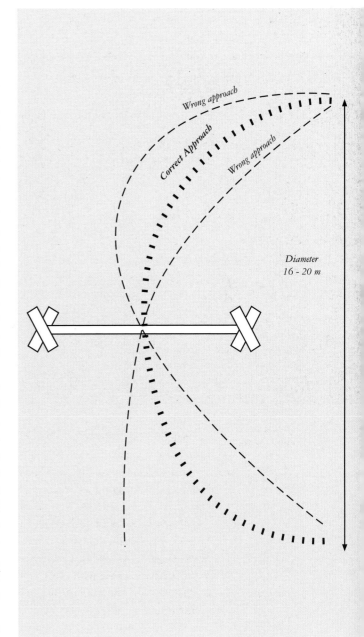

It is important to bend the horse correctly in a circle when approaching a fence from a circle.

With a correct approach, horse and rider are more likely to find a good take-off distance to the fence.
Photo: Hölscher

preferable to approach a horse from the inside rather than from the outside. The horse's position and bend to the inside during the approach means that it is very likely to land on the inside leg (correct canter) if it has been exercised regularly on both reins. If not, the rider needs to learn to decide whether he is going to correct the horse immediately on landing, or let the horse continue in counter-canter if the following fence is very close. This is an important factor in jumping courses at a later stage. If jumping an individual jump on a circle, it is better to correct the horse's canter immediately, so it has sufficient time to concentrate on the renewed approach of the jump. Changing the canter can either be executed as a flying change or by slowing down to a trot and cantering on again on the other leg.

Several jumps in a row should be executed on a circle. In the beginning, it is not easy to rearrange one's seat and correct the length of the reins and concentrate on approaching the next fence on the circle at the same time. This requires practice and more practice. If one rider in the group has difficulties with his horse, it may be advisable for him to ride the circle on his own.

On a circle, the outer hand in particular has to give over the fence in order to maintain the bend of the horse to the inside. The inner rein maintains a slight bend to the inside over the jump, but must not inhibit the freedom of the horse's head and neck during the jump. The rider's legs retain their position from the approach. These aids alone should be sufficient to encourage the horse to land on the correct foot. If the rider pulls the horse's head too far to the inside in order to force it to land correctly, the opposite will usually happen, as this tends to make the horse unbalanced.

JUMPING PARTS OF A COURSE

At first, the riders should jump a fence or a group of fences without refusals several times to get a feeling for riding a course. Jumping individual fences is easier, as the rider has time to stop his horse after a fence and ride it on the bit again. Once the rider has jumped several jumps without pause, he will learn to ride the horse back on the bit as early as possible after the landing and to correct its tempo.

Initially, the rider's concentration will lapse very quickly after the first two or three repeat courses, and consequently the jumping will get worse. After a while, the ability to concentrate over repeated jumps on the circle or on a straight line will improve.

Now is the time to start jumping simple obstacle courses. The rider learns to concentrate on the approach to the next fence. By now, the correct seat on the approach to and over the fence should come naturally. Corrections to the seat need to be made over individual fences and not when jumping courses.

Before jumping part of a course, it is worthwhile to make the riders dismount and walk the course, looking at the best routes to take between the fences. They should memorise the points where they have to turn or start a bend. This is also a useful preparation for walking an unfamiliar course. Once the correct line to take has been discussed, each rider should initially canter on the track or on a circle before starting the course. At this stage, I normally correct the tempo and rider's aids. If the horse is cantering correctly

*Walking the course
should be practised
right from the start.
Photo: Schmelzer*

on the bit, the rider should commence. He should concentrate primarily on finding the correct line and jumping each fence in the centre at a steady pace.

Turning in good time is an important factor in finding the correct line of approach to a jump. During jumping, the horse is turned towards the fence relatively early in order to prevent it from drifting too far out. When for example jumping a fence on the second track of the riding school, the horse should be turned towards the jump at the centre of the short side, or even earlier. Due to the less acute turn, the horse can then remain steadily on the bit during the entire approach and achieve the correct collection in front of the fence. Also, as discussed previously, the horse has the chance to drift slightly to the outside of the fence, to correct the take-off distance, if there is not enough room.

On a course, the rider needs to learn to concentrate solely on the next fence to jump.
Photo: Hermann

JUMPING COURSES

ABILITY TO CONCENTRATE

In time, more and more fences are added or the same fences ridden twice to practise jumping real courses and to improve the ability of both horse and rider to concentrate whilst jumping. The rider has to practise memorising the course and riding the horse into the correct position during the course.

In order to be able to memorise the course, the rider needs to visualise the correct sequence of jumps and know without looking which fence follows next, what it looks like and how to approach it. The more frequently he practises this with different courses, the better he will be able to memorise the right sequence at a show or during a competition.

In my lessons, I often set up a course with up to fifteen fences to school the riders. In this case, however, the fences should be kept low, as the rider should be concentrating on finding the right way, and a course with many higher fences would be too difficult at this stage. In an indoor arena, the fences can be jumped twice or from both directions, if there is lack of space.

*If horse and rider have the right basic tempo during the approach to a fence, the result will be a harmonic, calm jump over the obstacle.
Photo: S. Stuewer*

THE BASIC TEMPO

The correct basic tempo is dependent on the speed offered by the horse. The ideal is a lively, well co-ordinated canter with the horse on the bit and its hindquarters engaged. Cantering too slowly and sluggishly means that the horse will have insufficient impulse and speed to jump the fences.

If the tempo, on the other hand, becomes too fast, there is the danger that the horse "falls apart" and can no longer be controlled by its rider. This is extremely dangerous and when riding a course, the rider needs to be urged to get back to a good, steady tempo by riding on the track or on a circle, before continuing to jump. There is a good chance that the horse will refuse, if it approaches the fence at too high a speed. In addition, there is the risk that the horse will fall at the fence or in a turn, if the speed is too rushed.

The rushed (uncontrollable) tempo also makes it far more difficult to judge the take-off at the fences, as the stride lengthens when the horse increases its speed and it becomes difficult to get the strides right. Later, when riding in competitions the rider will also often have the problem that, faced with an unfamiliar fence, the horse will become nervous if it is rushing the fence at too much speed. It should have the chance to have a look at the fence for as long as possible.

Naturally, the right tempo will have been practised again and again when jumping individual fences. A lively basic tempo, with the horse on the bit and engaging its hindquarters well, is ideal. It is of extreme importance when jumping fences that the horse engages its hindquarters well, as the engaged hindquarters are the main factor which allows the horse to push itself off the ground with the necessary force.

During the course, the rider needs to increase the tempo between the fences again and again and slow down during the approach in order to achieve sufficient thrust with the hindquarters. The motto in this case is "from the higher speed to the lower speed" in front of the fence, which predominantly means the lengthening and shortening of the stride. The horse should be on the bit, obeying the rider's aids all the time and should remain under control at all times. When increasing speed the rider needs to ensure that he does not simply throw away the reins, but that, as for the medium canter, the horse is slowly pushed increasingly onto the bit by the rider's seat and the rider then gives the reins, millimetre by millimetre, thus lengthening the stride at the canter.

One difficulty when riding show jumping courses is that the horse can "fall apart" or escape the rider's aids between fences. During schooling sessions, it is important to repeatedly ride fence sequences, and if the horse no longer responds to the aids or if the tempo is not ideal, to ride in circles in order to get the horse back under control, before continuing with the course. Turning away to ride a circle should however be avoided immediately before an obstacle, or course, so as not to teach the horse to refuse. Soon after landing, the rider has to decide whether to commence jumping or whether to correct the horse's tempo first.

Just as in dressage, the posture of the horse needs to be improved for show jumping. It needs to engage its hindquarters increasingly at the canter and lengthen or shorten its stride at the slightest aids, which is of extreme importance for judging the take-off. For this purpose, it is recommended to repeatedly ride exercises whereby the rider lengthens and shortens the horse's stride at the canter around the fences. The better and more precisely horse and rider work together, the easier it is to jump a course.

LEVEL OF SCHOOLING OF THE SHOW JUMPER

Naturally, the horse has to be on the bit when jumping a course. During the gymnastic jumping and jumping from the trot, we prefer the horse to stretch forwards and downward, as this is the optimum way to loosen the back muscles and to achieve as many rounded fences with as good a bascule as possible. When approaching a fence at the canter, the forwards and downward position of the horse is not ideal. It should become more upright in front of a fence so that the rider has the horse's neck in front of him and is able to control the canter strides. Also the horse needs to engage its hindquarters increasingly, in order to be able to take off with sufficient impulsion.

Horses which carry their head too low when approaching a fence may have a tendency to canter with the weight on the forehand and not to push their front legs off the ground fast and high enough. A remedy for this fault is to ride the horse uphill at a collected pace, making sure that it still uses its back. In between the fences the horse is ridden with a lower head position again and in a rounded canter.

Ideally the horse will flex its poll correctly during jumping. There are, however, many horses which prefer to raise their heads above the reins when approaching a fence. Although it would

The better the horse obeys the rider's aids in front of a fence, the more harmonious the take-off will be. Photo: Schmelzer

certainly be more comfortable if the horse flexed its poll throughout, the rider should not force the horse in such a situation. It is perfectly accept-able for the horse to raise its head and neck as long as it continues to obey the aids and rounds its back. What the rider should avoid at all times is forcing down the horse's head in between the fences by pulling the reins alternately. During gymnastic exercises, the rider of a horse with such tendencies should make sure that his horse moves forwards and downward freely, in order to prevent the occurrence of back problems, which would then mean that the horse will no longer jump willingly.

COMPETITIONS AND SHOWS

To ensure that riders are well prepared for competitions, they should also practise the correct way to enter the arena and greet the judges. For this purpose, a start and finish line are set up and the position of the imaginary judges is determined. Now the rider practises entering the arena without crossing the start line. He is allowed to trot once around the course towards the judges, but should avoid drawn-out circling around all fences. In this way he can trot past a difficult fence to familiarise the horse with it. It is however prohibited to show the fences to the horse before jumping the course. Therefore the rider needs to ensure that he does not ride too close to any fence. Showing a horse a fence is allowed only after a refusal. After trotting around the course, the rider then comes to a halt facing the judges and drops his hand in greeting.

It is not necessary to halt directly in front of the judges' box, but on the other hand the rider should not halt too far away so that the judges are unable to see the competitor's number.

After the greeting, the rider pushes the horse into a trot and then immediately into a canter. The rider should have a close look at the line between the greeting point and the start line when he walks the course. Thus he will be able to avoid crossing the start line too early, and being disqualified. Approaching the start line, the rider should adopt the forward seat. In a jumping competition judged on style (not common in this country), the judges will take note of this and it is possible to achieve points at this stage.

At the end of the course, horse and rider have to cross the finish line. This should also be noted during course walking, in order to avoid getting three faults for a refusal for having to ride a circle to cross the finish line, or worse, of being disqualified for not having crossed the finish line, in the excitement and heat of the moment.

FLYING CHANGES AT THE CANTER

Once the rider starts jumping courses, he should start working on flying changes at the canter with his horse. To teach the horse to change legs during practice, I usually place individual poles in the arena in such a way that the horse has to ride over these poles in the form of a serpentine when changing the leg, in the same way as changing the leg from one circle to the other in a figure of eight. Here, the rider learns to bend his horse in the new direction one stride in front of the pole. Only then, does he change the position of his lower legs and pushes the new inner seat bone forward to initiate the flying change. It is important that the aids are given calmly and in the right order.

Bending the horse the other way and changing the position of the rider's legs at the same time only confuses the horse. The rider remains sitting deeply in the saddle and does not stand in the stirrups. It is often a very useful aid to trigger the flying change by clicking one's tongue, which is more easily understood by the horse than the use of spurs or the whip.

If the horse persistently refuses to change legs, the rider should slow the horse down to a trot for a moment shortly after the pole and then ask it to canter again on the right leg. This exercise should be practised time and time again until the horse understands what the rider wants it to do. Sometimes this can take weeks. It is a simple case of having to be patient. At some stage the horse will execute a flying change and it should then be praised and rewarded profusely.

Often the horse will change the front legs but not the hind legs and keep on cantering disunitedly, which is immediately noticeable due to the discomfort it causes the rider. In this case, the rider must try to encourage the horse to also change its hind legs directly behind the pole by giving the horse repeated clear aids in the bend to carry out the transition from the trot to the canter on the inside leg. An important factor in this exercise is the necessity to set the limit for the horse with the out-

side aids so that it does not swing out. If the horse fails to change legs immediately, the rider needs to slow down to a trot once more and repeat the transition to the correct canter. Then the horse should be praised. The shorter the trotting stage the easier it is for the horse to associate the aids with what the rider requires it to do. Avoid overdoing it, however, as the horse will only become upset and excited or even panic when practising flying changes at the canter. In this case, it is impossible for the horse to change legs correctly.

If the horse consistently refuses to change legs on one side, it will almost certainly not have been made supple equally on both sides. The change of legs on one side is always as good as the degree to which the horse can bend to this side and engage its hindquarters correctly. Increasing suppling exercises on the stiffer side will in time also solve the problem of the flying change at the canter.

The rider introduces the flying change over the pole on the ground by bending the horse the other way and using the new inner leg to create impulsion. Photo: C. Busch

35

Here, relieving the weight on the horse's back by means of the forward seat is demonstrated at the halt. Photo: C. Busch

JUMPING SEAT ON THE COURSE

I would now like to clarify the ongoing discussion of whether to ride the entire course in the jumping seat or not.

Between the fences the horse should be ridden in the jumping seat as a matter of principle in order to relieve the horse's back. During the approach to each fence, the rider however needs to sit more closely in the saddle in good time, maintaining the forward position, so he can control the strides of the horse with his seat. I don't think much of approaching fences in the jumping seat, as the rider has little influence on the horse and a refusal, in my opinion, is therefore practically pre-programmed even if the horse is a very confident jumper. It requires the balanced effect of the rider's weight before the jump for the horse to approach the fence with determination. If the horse decides to run out, the rider again can do little to prevent it.

If you watch high-level jumping competitions, you will notice that all riders sit down in the saddle to a greater or lesser degree in front of a fence in order to keep their horses under control. The level of schooling of the horse determines to what degree the rider has to sit into the saddle. Horses which have a tendency to pull against the reins and start rushing in front of a fence, require a deeper seat and a more upright position of the rider's upper body, to enable him to shorten the stride and set the horse up for the jump. Lazy horses also require more weight in the saddle so that the rider can push it forward.

That said, the rider should keep his upper body in the forward position so as not to get left behind during take-off. A few horses react with such sensitivity to the aids in front of a fence that the forward seat is almost comparable to the jumping seat. The rider however should make sure that his seat bones have light contact with the saddle. After the fence the rider then remains in the jumping seat until he approaches the next fence, unless the next fence follows immediately. After the landing phase the rider then adopts the jumping seat again. When tackling sharp corners, especially in indoor schools, the rider should also sit deeper in the saddle to prevent the horse from losing its balance and falling.

The rider changes from forward to jumping seat and back in order to stay in optimum harmony with the horse in the combination. Photo: A. Busch

ADVANCED SHOW JUMPING

SEAT AND RIDER'S INFLUENCE

Once the foundations for show jumping have been laid and strengthened, it is time to further improve the technique and effect of the rider's aids. To begin with, we again concentrate on the rider's seat. So far, the rider has learned to go with the horse's movement and to give it sufficient freedom. Now the aids at and over the jump are

further refined. In order to be able to jump higher fences with the horse, it is important that the rider learns to put more energy into the tempo of the horse during the last few strides before the fence, so that the horse will take off with more impulsion. The rider sits down as if he wants to push the horse into the medium canter, but at the same time gently holds in the impulsion created by the back and legs, with the reins. This ensures that the increased energy is used by the horse to engage its hindquarters and place them further under its body, allowing it to take off with greater force. On the approach to wide oxers, it is important to set up the horse and create more energy for the jump.

Now, the rider also learns not to start taking his weight off the horse's back until the moment of take-off. In the past, he learned to fold forward

In order to jump a wider oxer, it is important to approach the fence with plenty of impulsion. Photo: S. Stuewer

For very sensitive horses, a bitless bridle such as the hackamore may be an alternative to the normal loose ring snaffle.
Photo: S. Stuewer

the reins over the fence. So far, of course, he was taught to let the reins hang in loops over the fence. Now the rider maintains contact with the horse's mouth, but moves forward sufficiently with his hands so that the horse has the opportunity to stretch to the optimum over the fence. Up to the moment of take-off the rider maintains a flexible connection with the horse's mouth and places his hands in such a position at the actual take-off that the reins can follow the horse's mouth like an elastic band. The hands should be positioned with slight contact to the horse's neck on either side of the neck or on the crest.

Under no circumstances must the rider pull at the reins. The hands should remain completely independent, so that they can be taken forward by the horse's mouth without any feeling of resistance when the horse stretches its neck forward.

During the landing phase, the reins are slowly shortened again until the horse is straight back on the bit with a shortened neck after the landing, and the rider has the correct amount of contact to approach the following fence. Retaining contact with the horse's mouth during the moment of suspension over the fence is imperative when jumping higher and complicated combinations. Very often, the horse has to be collected and set up immediately after the fence, if the approach to the next fence is short. If the rider has to work on regaining contact with the horse's mouth after landing, it will be too late to influence the horse. Many horses also jump cleaner if they have slightly more contact during the take-off and suspension, as long as the rein does not interfere with the horse.

with his upper body a bit earlier in order not to get left behind. Now he must recognise the take-off line and rise in the saddle at the same moment that the horse takes off.

The best place to practise this is grids, as the rider is able to concentrate on his seat without approaching any fence with an awkward stride.

Once the rider has learned to stay with the horse during the jump every time and there is no danger that he will interfere with the horse's mouth, it is time to learn to keep contact with

THE CORRECT BIT

In principle, I am of the opinion that a horse should be ridden on a normal loose ring snaffle, if necessary with a running martingale. If the rider's contact with the horse's mouth is not satisfactory with the snaffle, the best thing to do is to continue schooling the horse on the flat (dressage) until it is supple and receptive enough to stay on the bit at all times. In exceptional circumstances, this will not be possible, and it is then practical to use a different kind of bit, which is in fact allowed in competitions. The best bits for this purpose are a kimberwick or a pelham, which however do have the disadvantage that horses ridden with these bits tend to refuse more quickly, if the rider uses too much force with his hands. Therefore, more severe bits should be used with caution and belong only in the hands of experienced riders if they are to be used at all. Despite being jumped in these bits, the horse should continue to be schooled with a normal snaffle, and the rider should try to improve the horse's responsiveness to the restraining aids.

Unfortunately, many show jumping riders use draw reins. Under no circumstances should a horse be jumped in draw reins, due to the extreme danger of a serious fall if the take-off is judged incorrectly. Consistent flat-work schooling of the horse to willingly obey the rider's aids cannot be replaced by pulling the horse's head down and in with draw reins. Quite the contrary: the horse will resist the draw reins by tensing the muscles on the lower neck and will pull even more against the rider's hands, once the draw reins have been removed.

JUDGING THE TAKE-OFF

Judging the take-off means finding the correct take-off line in front of a fence. This is referred to as the rider having an "eye" for the take-off. Some riders have a gift for seeing the correct distances for the take-off. Others have to learn this ability through consistent

With its final stride, the horse should arrive at the ideal take-off line for the fence.

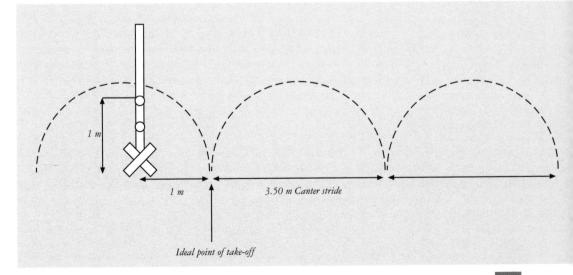

1 m

1 m   3.50 m Canter stride

Ideal point of take-off

schooling. The horse is only able to lift itself off the ground and over the fence at the end of a canter stride. The jump over the fence is a basically a bigger canter stride. At the same time, it is important that the horse takes off at the correct point in front of a jump. For an upright fence, the ideal take-off line is as far away from the fence as the fence is high; when jumping a spread, the take-off line is slightly closer. When jumping smaller fences, it makes no difference really if the take-off distance before the fence varies by up to 50 centimetres in either direction. The horse can jump in this entire area without the jump becoming awkward or causing the horse to make errors. However, the higher the jump and the less jumping ability the horse possesses, the more accurately the horse must hit the take-off line in order to jump the fence without a fault. If the last stride before the fence ends before the correct take-off line, the horse will either try to take off early or try to fit in an extra stride which will lead to an unsteady stride and a take-off far too close to the fence. Horses which are cautious by nature or wich have had bad experiences may refuse in such a case. If the horse's last stride before the fence ends too close to the obstacle, it only has the option of taking off too close to the fence or refusing, especially if the fence is high. In this case, it will most likely dislodge a pole with its front legs if it jumps. The pre-requisite for correct judging of the take-off line is an obedient, responsive horse, so that the rider can take the horse to the take-off line he has determined.

Walking Distances Between Fences

The rider should school himself to walk with a stride of one metre in order to be able to measure the distances between the fences. For this purpose, the length of one metre is measured with a measuring stick and the rider impresses on his mind how long his stride must be to measure one metre. Then further distances are measured and the rider walks the distance, for example 7 metres or 10.5 metres in any combination. Half a stride equates to 50 centimetres. The rider should repeatedly practise walking with the correct length of stride, as it is of utmost importance when setting up fences and when walking the course with its unfamiliar distances at a show.

At the same time, the rider needs to learn the possible distances for combinations and related distances in order to be able to decide whether the distance between two fences fits or is either wide or narrow. At a show, this is of extreme importance when the courses get more difficult, in order to match the horse's stride accordingly. Of course, this also means that the rider has to know the length of the stride at the canter of his horse. In combinations, the distance between fences usually lies at around 7 metres or around 10.5 metres (one stride or two strides). In related distances the distance between the fences is around 14 metres or 17.5 metres (three strides or four strides). The length of a normal horse's stride at the canter is between 3 metres and 4.50 metres.

Recognising the Take-off Line

Recognising the distance for take-off (even of an incorrect one) is the first step to getting a feel for judging the take-off. For this purpose, the take-off line should be marked in front of the fence. The rider can then concentrate on this line during the approach and decide after the jump whether he took off before the line (too early), behind it (too late) or correctly on it. With practice the rider will also learn to decide at what distance to the fence his horse should take off, without the help of a marked line, and how he should approach the fence. At this stage, the rider should under no circumstances attempt to slow down the horse to hit the take-off line precisely, as this will teach him to ride "backwards" in front of a fence and the horse will lose too much impulsion.

Judging the Take-Off in Grids

Now is the time to practise judging the take-off in grids. This will make it clear to the rider, how a bad take-off at the first fence of a combination will have an effect on the subsequent fences. Experience and knowledge of these correlations will help him greatly later on so that he can compensate for an incorrect take-off into a combination with the correct aids and thereby prevent faults or a refusal.

To practise this, you need to set up a grid to be jumped from the canter. In the beginning, a take-off line can be drawn in front of the first fence. To begin with, the rider again needs to recognise the correct distance.

Each jumping sequence should be discussed. If the take-off for the first fence was too close or lacked impulsion, the following distances will become wide. To compensate for this, the rider needs to push his horse forwards at the next fence. In the case of an early and wide take-off, the horse will land

Take-off poles in front of the fence help the rider get a feel for the correct take-off distance.
Photo: S. Stuewer

with plenty of impulsion well after the fence and will almost certainly come too close to the second obstacle. Here, the rider will have to pull back his horse slightly in order to retain sufficient space for jumping.

The most important thing is that the rider should not be afraid of misjudging the take-off line. No rider can get this right to begin with and it simply takes time to learn. But every rider can and must learn it in order to be able to jump difficult fences.

A further positive side-effect is that the rider will now understand why horses will sometimes take off awkwardly and the rider will get left behind. In the past they will have blamed the horse for this, now they understand that it is they who are not yet able to ride the horse into a good position for the take-off. Learning to understand one's horse is one of the most important points in show jumping and needs to be practised from the start, because only a rider who can put himself in the place of his horse will give the correct aids and will ensure that the horse retains its enthusiasm for jumping.

Setting Up Combinations and Related Distances

When approaching a combination of an upright fence followed by an oxer, it is ideal to jump into the combination with normal impulsion, either at the correct take-off line or slightly earlier (the horse should always stand back a bit in front of uprights and take off closer in front of spreads). Then the rider pushes his horse forwards energetically with his seat to jump the oxer. This ensures on the one hand that the horse comes a bit closer to the spread fence and that it also gains increased impulsion to be able to jump the oxer. If you have a horse with a big stride, it is better to jump the upright closer with less impulsion and then approach the oxer without increased pressure.

If the first fence in a combination is a spread followed by an upright, the task is more difficult. To jump the oxer successfully, the horse has to be ridden with plenty of impulsion, which will mean that it will land further into the combination. This can mean that it will get too close to the following

When jumping into a combination, the rider should maintain a sensitive contact with the horse's mouth. Photo: Jahraus

upright and will risk a fault. There-fore, the rider needs to sit up immedia-tely upon landing after the oxer and use his back, legs and reins to restrain the horse and shorten the canter stride. The aids are similar to a transition from the canter to the trot, and the rider sits deep and gently restrains the forward impulsion of the horse with his reins. At the same time, he must keep the horse cantering. The restrain-ing influence of the reins must not be too strong, as this would cause the horse to press down its back and resist the rider. In the ideal situation, the rider will maintain a flexible connec-tion to the horse's mouth at the moment of suspension.

Of course, the same theory applies to related distances as well. Here horse and rider have three or four strides bet-ween each fence. This means on the one hand that the rider has a bit more space to influence the stride of his horse, but on the other hand there is a danger with several strides that a horse cante-ring normally will arrive incorrectly at the next take-off line due to having put in a short or a long stride. Therefore, riders should practise collecting their horses between the fences in related distance combinations and approa-ching the next fence as a new obstacle. For this purpose he sits deep in the saddle after the landing phase of the preceding jump and concentrates on the next fence until he finds the correct take-off line.

Distances Around Corners

Here, the line to take between the fen-ces is slightly bent, and it is therefore not possible to determine the exact number of strides. The line that the rider decides to take will determine the number of strides. In these combinati-ons the rider must not rely on the number of strides determined during the walking of the course, but has to judge the take-off line anew for the fol-lowing fence.

It is also important that the horse is responsive to the rider's aids and bends willingly. After the landing phase, the horse is bent with the inside lower leg on the girth. The inside leg enlarges the bend, if necessary, the outside lower leg keeps the horse from swing-ing out its hindquarters and tightens the bend, if required. The rider should avoid turning the horse around sharply for a correct approach of the next fence.

How to Judge the Take-Off

Judging the take-off line for each fence is primarily a matter of concentration and a lot of practising. To start off with, the rider should approach an individual fence. He concentrates sole-ly on the fence and does not take his eyes of it until the moment of take-off. The problem of insufficient concentra-tion is particularly evident at unfamili-ar show grounds, where riders can be so distracted that sometimes they fail to see the take-off line, although jud-ging the take-off has worked perfectly in schooling sessions.

The rider practises to look at the take-off line on the ground before the fence and to influence the pace of his horse in such a manner that it is able to take off at precisely the line envisa-ged. Some riders prefer looking at the top pole of the fence. This is a matter of opinion. I myself look at the take-off line on the ground in front of the fence

Total concentration is needed for successfully judging the distance when jumping a course.
Photo: Stuewer

or shorten its stride in order to arrive at the fence in the ideal position. At all times the rider keeps his legs on the horse and drives it forward. The rider must not forget to shorten his horse and set it up approximately ten to fifteen metres before the fence and to concentrate on the point of take-off.

To begin with, the rider will only be able to see the correct distance before the fence very late, often only one or two strides before. In time, he should recognise the correct take-off line further and further away and thereby ideally support his horse during the approach phase. The rider should continue to practise judging the correct take-off, time and time again, so he will see the correct spot ever earlier.

During schooling sessions, the rider should steadily increase the number of jumps where he has judged the take-off correctly. He should not however put himself under too much pressure, as only the very top show jumping riders are able to approach each fence at the correct distance. For everybody else, the percentage of correctly judged fences will increase, the better the rider rides. Most horses easily forgive one misjudged take-off, it is only repeated badly judged mishaps which will have a negative effect on them.

because it does not really matter how high and wide a fence is, as long as I approach it with sufficient impulsion and tell the horse to take off at the right moment. The horse needs to look at the fence and prepare his jump accordingly. The rider's influence on the pace and stride must be a forward driving aid. It is wrong to set up the horse in front of a fence to such a degree that it is practically cantering on the spot, and arrives at the correct distance to the fence but without any spring and impulsion whatsoever. All the top riders are able to judge the take-off perfectly at a free-moving tempo. To judge the take-off line, the horse is simply encouraged to lengthen

Taking Off too Close too Frequently

If the rider finds that he and his horse arrive too close to the jump too often, it is more than likely that the rider is shortening the horse's stride in front of the fence too much and is using his hands too severely. In this way, he almost rides the horse "under" the fence. To correct this mistake, the rider has to increase his tempo and ride

The slightly advanced ground line established by the barrels and the pole, prevents the horse from taking off too close. Photo: C. Busch

towards the fence with more impulsion. This causes the horse to lengthen its stride and it is able to take off earlier. I also recommend this corrective measure during the jumping of a course. If the rider has realised that he has come too close to a fence several times, he should increase the overall speed and ask his horse to engage its hindquarters more actively, so that it does not always have to take off with too little impulsion. Often this can prevent a refusal long before the fence looms.

If the horse does not stand back in front of a fence and take off earlier despite having been ridden forwards with good impulsion, it will have to be led to the correct take-off line with appropriate gymnastic exercises. As always, we are talking of a healthy horse where the cause is not a matter of ill-health. To encourage the horse to stand back more from the fence, a

pole can be laid in front of the fence to encourage the horse to take off earlier.

Taking Off too Soon too Frequently

If the horse tends to jump early, its stride is probably too long. This can be caused by insufficient schooling or by the rider's influence. In the case of very wide oxers, for example, jumping off too early often means that the horse cannot jump wide enough to clear the fence cleanly. It will either jump too high or rap its hindlegs on the final pole of the oxer. Both options are painful and will make the horse feel insecure, so that it will refuse to jump from this distance.

The counter-measure for the rider is to set up his horse better on approach and collect it. He needs to shorten the horse's strides and push the horse almost up to the fence. You can also achieve this result by placing a pole on the ground as a take-off aid.

Judging the Take-Off Coming out of a Turn

The fences in a course cannot always be approached from a straight line. Very often, the rider will have to approach the next fence coming out of a turn. Although this may seem more difficult for riders to begin with, it is actually easier, once horse and rider have become accustomed to it. When forced to ride a turn, the rider can influence the approach to the take-off line by riding a larger or smaller turn. Arriving at the fence in a diagonal position, the horse is able to compensate for coming too close by slightly drifting out. Also, a long straight approach to a fence is not ideal for the psyche of horse and rider. On the one hand, the route is long enough to produce insecurity as to whether one will get the distance right, on the other hand most horses start rushing the next fence, if they can see it a long way off and often escape the rider's hands and legs

When approaching a fence out of a turn, it is important to focus on the approach of the next fence during the turn, to ride the horse collectedly on the bit and to wait for the correct take-off distance. It is easier to collect a horse in a turn than on a straight line, and facilitates the approach.

For practising purposes, a fence is put up on the circle or on the diagonal line across the whole school. It is then moved nearer and nearer to the turning point, until horse and rider have to jump the fence directly out of the corner. This, of course, is initially practised with a low fence, later with higher fences.

Improving the Ability of the Horse to Judge the Take-Off

In an ideal situation, the horse and rider support each other and judge the correct take-off line together. Horses which have had schooling in free jumping lessons are often very much better able to compensate an incorrect approach and take-off. In most cases, they will come back to hand of their own accord in front of the fence (that means they seek contact with the rider's hands and wait) and are therefore also easier to ride to the correct take-off. Some horses are even able to fit in an extra half cantering stride, if the take-off would otherwise have been completely impossible. When approaching a fence correctly, this should not be necessary of course, but it is an advantage, if the horse can help the rider out of a messy situation.

In addition to free jumping sessions, the rider should also support the horse's independent co-operation at a fence with a number of exercises under the saddle. The rider can, for example, approach a small fence without indicating to the horse when to take off. The

Special stands for the boards around an indoor school, can be used to set up effective grids for the purpose of judging the take-off.
Photo: C. Busch

horse is merely kept on the bit and encouraged to jump by being steadily driven forwards towards the fence. If the horse accepts the fence willingly and takes off at a reasonable distance, the rider lightens his contact to the horse's mouth until the reins hang slack. The horse is however prevented from falling apart by the forward driving leg and back aids. The rider does not judge the distance to the take-off line. You will have to proceed very carefully step by step in this exercise in order not to knock the horse's confidence and make it feel insecure. Horses which have difficulties with this should initially approach the fence from a trot.

In time, talented horses will almost always come to the fence correctly and at the same time the rider gets a feeling for the basic tempo that the horse is comfortable with and the rhythm in which it prefers to jump a fence. The rider should adapt to this. Naturally,

these exercises only supplement the schooling process and should only be carried out from time to time and always over small fences, where the risk of anything happening is negligible. If you have a horse which pulls and rushes its fences, it is wise to lengthen the reins only marginally, bit by bit. On the other hand, these horses also profit from the independent approach to the fence, as they will often become calmer, if they are not held back in front of a fence. In the beginning they will come up to the fence too fast or too close and have to make an effort to jump. If the rider is lucky, the horse will react to this, will in future gather itself together more in front of the fence and can be collected more easily. For this exercise, the speed should only be corrected by means of the voice and, if necessary, (as too great a speed is dangerous) with short, light rein aids. Pulling on the reins should be avoided at all costs.

Here, horse and rider have judged the ideal distance in front of the fence for take-off.
Photo: Jahraus

The solid fillers help horse and rider judge the take-off.
Photo: Hölscher

EXTERNAL CONDITIONS WHICH AFFECT THE TAKE-OFF

Getting the take-off right, of course, is also dependent on the temperament and pace at the canter of the horse, and on external conditions such as fence type, state of the ground and general environment. Normally, the rider should always ride the same horse in order to be able to achieve an optimum understanding with it.

Take-Off Problems of the Horse

Depending on their temperament, horses have the tendency either to become excitable in front of a fence, and therefore to take off too early, or slightly too lazy, thereby getting too close. One should not however generalise these tendencies, as they are also dependent on the length of the horse's stride at the canter and its preference of how to jump a fence.

One has to find out as a matter of principle what kind of difficulties the horse experiences when tackling fences. Horses which under no circumstances want to stand back in front of an oxer, as they would then possibly be unable to clear the fence, need to be ridden closer to all spread fences. The rider needs to practise this by using a take-off pole in front of a fence and moving it closer and closer to the fence, to give the horse the feeling for the correct take-off line and to give the rider the feeling for the correct distance. Later, a mark which shows the rider where the horse should take off, can help the him judge the correct take-off distance.

Very often, this means adapting to a different way of jumping a fence, as the rider may have got used to his horse taking off too early and now subjectively feels that the correct take-off line is too close to the fence.

Horses which constantly get too close for take-off at upright fences need to be taught with a pole on the ground in front of the fence which is moved further back, bit by bit, to stand back from the fence and take off at the correct distance. The take-off pole however must not be placed too far in front of the fence, as the horse will take it for a trotting pole and put its feet in the space between the pole and the fence. In-outs can also be widened or shortened in front of a fence ad lib to bring horse and rider into the ideal take-off position.

Ground Line

The ground line of the fence is the foremost line of the fence on the ground, for example a brush filler or the lowest pole. Pulling the ground pole slightly forward makes it easier for horse and rider to judge the take-off line. Due to the horse's restricted field of vision it becomes more difficult for the horse if the ground line is missing, disrupted or has been pulled underneath the fence, for example in a wall with an open arc in the middle. Placing a flower pot in the open arc makes judging the take-off easier again. The rider should take particular note when walking the course where such a ground line is not available so he can collect the horse together more in front of that particular fence. Jumps which do not have any fillers and have plenty of air under the top pole are not as inviting for a horse to jump as fences with solid fillers and plenty of closely placed poles. At home, the rider should practise jumping very airy looking fences, for

example a fence of around one metre with only two poles placed closely together.

In novice competitions, a false ground line, i.e. one set back beneath the fence, should not be incorporated into the course as the horse will thus be tricked into misjudging the take-off

A flimsy looking pole with airy gaps is more difficult to judge and jump clear.
Photo: Giers

Jumping individual poles at a low height improves the ability of the horse to judge the take-off line.
Photo: Hermann

A horse can more easily see poles with distinct colour contrasts, such as these in black and white, than unicoloured poles. Photo: Hermann

line. They do however occur in advanced competitions, or as the joker in a high-scoring class. It is almost impossible for the horse to judge the fence due to the ground line lying further away than the top poles. This is where refusals will almost invariably occur, if the rider fails to pay special attention.

Colours of the Fences

Horses see colours differently from people. Their colour spectrum is significantly smaller. In part, all they can make out are contrasts. For this reason, most jumps are painted in traditional white and one other colour. The horse is able to see these well. Dark fences, such as natural cross-country fences are difficult for horses to see and they find it difficult to judge the take-off line. Therefore, these fences often present problems. Therefore, you should take care to practise natural fences extensively at home. At a show the horse will need extra help at such fences, if one is included in the course.

The general rule is: the less intense the contrast between dark and light colours of the poles, the more difficult it is to jump the fence. Another thing to take into account is the background behind the fence. A white fence in front of a white background, for example, is particularly difficult. This is also the reason why some horses always experience problems with certain coloured fences. These problems can only be resolved if the rider has the patience to increase the trust between him and his horse through schooling.

Natural cross-country fences are particularly difficult for the horse to see.
Photo: C. Busch

Ground Conditions

Naturally, the state of the ground also influences how the horse and rider approach a fence. You should therefore practise on as many different types of surface as possible. Grass and sand are the most common surfaces found and definitely form a part of the training repertoire of every rider (and horse). In extremely deep going, much of the horse's momentum is absorbed so that the rider needs to increase his horse's basic tempo in order to achieve the desired result. He will have to drive the horse forwards with increased impulsion in order to approach the fence at the correct stride, once he has recognised the position of the take-off line. The horse also needs the additional momentum to be able to jump high enough on deep going. If the ground is flat and very springy, the rider may have to reduce the speed slightly.

Jumping Uphill and Downhill

Jumping uphill lengthens the effective distance of the take-off line, i.e., the rider needs to ride with more impulsion and speed to arrive at the fence correctly. The gradient absorbs momentum and requires the rider to ride with far more energy and stronger aids. In addition, he should take into account that the horse should not stand too far back from the fence, as an uphill fence requires the horse to jump higher and wider than on the level. Jumping downhill, the reverse applies so that the rider needs to anticipate the horse taking off early, or even to encourage the horse to do so. The rider does not lean as far forward over a downhill

The condition of the ground influences the requirements for the approach to a fence.
Photo: A. Busch

fence as he would on the level, in order not to unbalance the horse. When landing on a downward slope, the rider needs to focus his attention on sitting upright again as early as possible and to lean back more.

Other Influences

There are many different things on a show jumping course which have an influence on the horse. Basically horses find it easier to jump fences which are pointing in the direction of the entrance/exit and will tend to pull more towards those fences than towards those facing the opposite way. Therefore, fences facing away from the entrance/exit need to be ridden with extra impulsion. Fences facing the exit need to be taken with more restraint, especially if they happen to consist of a combination.

Jumping in an indoor school is very different from jumping outdoors. Across country or in the outdoor arena (school), horses are always more energetic and canter with greater momentum than in the often narrow indoor school. This must be taken into account when planning the approach to a fence.

In addition, what the fences look like is also important. Large solid obstacles such as walls, oxers with fillers and triple bars (Jacob's ladders) induce the horse to come back on the bit by itself, in other words, it approaches them with greater hesitation and sets itself up more. The rider should respond to this by driving the horse forwards energetically. Flimsily built, low fences, on the other hand tend to lead the horse to jump too fast and too flat. In these cases, the rider will have to collect his horse and shorten it.

Light conditions and the pressure of other horses in the vicinity of the course also influence the horse's behaviour. The rider should always take these factors into account. He always needs to try to see things through the eyes of his horse and to anticipate in advance how his horse will react. To practise this, the rider should stand in front of the fence and copy the visual angle of the horse, by placing his flat hand in front of his nose. The horse has its eyes to the right and left of the head and is unable to see what is directly in front of it without a visual block. This also impairs its spatial view.

Naturally, with time and experience, the rider will be able to estimate a course correctly when walking it, drawing on a vast amount of prior situations. Once the rider has made decisions about riding the course, he should not waver and throw them out once he is riding, as this would cause insecurity and a loss of concentration.

JUMPING WITHOUT FAULTS

Judging the correct take-off line is the deciding factor in jumping fences without incurring any faults. Most faults are the result of an incorrect take-off. In this matter, it is up to the rider to train his eye for the correct distance. Another important point is the way the rider applies his aids at the fence. If he remains too rigid with his hands at the moment of take-off, the horse will not arch its back and thereby not tuck in its legs far enough. This usually results in a dislodged pole. This can be observed very often, when the rider tries to steer his horse into the new direction while they are still in suspension over the fence.

In advanced, high jumping classes, you can observe that the riders will take up the rein again at the moment of take-off. In some horses, the short-term co-ordination of the aids in front of the fence (half-halt) results in a very pronounced rounding of the back and tucking in of the legs. The rider, however, should only use this method if he arrives at the fence correctly and does not disturb the horse during the moment of suspension, as it could otherwise make his mount lose confidence. The rider must not fail to give the reins even a second too late during take-off, as it will otherwise have the opposite effect altogether.

One good method to make the horse pay more attention is to close one's legs over the fence. This will make the horse more attentive and will cause it to jump with greater care.

Furthermore, the rider needs to make sure that the horse does not jump the fence too flat and leave its legs dangling. In most cases the reason for this is too much speed. The horse should be made to approach the horse in a more collected and rounded way.

Correction of Faults

If horse and rider have incurred a fault, it does not help if the rider punishes his horse, as it cannot, of course, differentiate between being punished for knocking down a pole for jumping as such. The correct way is to ride away from the fence with plenty of impulsion and to jump the same fence again immediately. If the horse jumps the fence faultlessly, it should be praised and then pulled up to a walk on the loose rein. If not, the fence should be taken again.

The rein-back can also be used as a corrective measure. After the horse has incurred a fault, the rider stops the horse and asks the horse for a few steps back. This is always seen as a punishment for the horse. Afterwards, the rider drives the horse forwards again and proceeds as detailed above. Horses which are trained in this way should be made to rein back before starting the course in an event such as a show. You will see many top riders do this. It will make the horse concentrate more during the task ahead.

Deliberate stepping over a single pole improves the attention of the horse.
Photo: C. Busch

Pole Work

When riding the horse over poles on the ground it is taught not to touch the poles. For this purpose, the horse is brought up to the bit increasingly while walking or trotting over the poles, and by repeating this exercise again and again until it no longer touches any of the poles. Afterwards it is praised lavishly and the exercise is terminated. The poles need to be laid out in such a way, however, that the horse will have no problems crossing them without incurring a fault.

Another useful aid is an individual pole which is raised on one side to a height of about 30 centimetres while resting on the ground on the other. Now the horse is slowly ridden step by step over the pole at the walk, first at the low end, later also in the centre of the pole. As soon as the horse performs this task well, in other words, lifts all its legs carefully over the pole, it should be praised and the exercise is terminated. The important thing here is the slow, deliberate picking up of each individual hoof. The rider can also stop for a split second between the front and the hind legs stepping over the pole in order to raise the attention of the horse.

Of course, all types of gymnastic jumping and grids are suitable to teach the horse to jump with care. Here, as always, the exercises are practised until the horse has jumped cleanly without a fault. What is important is to avoid lack of concentration on the part of the horse, by not forcing it to jump the same fences over and over again, but rather varying them continuously.

JUMPING HIGHER FENCES

Once the rider has become secure in giving the correct aids and influencing the horse over small fences, the time has come to slowly increase the demands of the height of the obstacles. This should not be attempted too early in the schooling phase of the rider however, as any excessive demands made at this stage will have a significantly negative effect on the psychological state of horse and rider.

With an increased height of the fences, the ideal take-off line moves further away from the fence. Therefore, judging the take-off for higher fences means that horse and rider have to adapt and become accustomed to the new situation. The correct approach towards higher fences needs to be schooled. In order to avoid meeting the fence wrong in the beginning, a small introduction fence is set up in front of the actual obstacle. Grids are particularly useful for this purpose. The "take-off jump" can be a cross-pole or even just a cavaletti. The important thing is that the horse gets the correct distance to the higher fence by jumping the small fence in front, and can then jump it from the right distance. This procedure increases the confidence of both horse and rider.

If the fences have been jumped faultlessly, they are raised or lowered. You should however always rest between schooling sessions with higher fences and jump smaller obstacles instead, in order to retain the trust of your horse. Not every jumping session can consist of jumping high fences. Even the top riders often school their horses with gymnastic exercises and only set up practical high fences occasionally, so as not to ask too much of their horses.

Higher fences at the end of a grid present no particular difficulty. The rider will have to drive his horse forwards with increased energy so he can ask the horse to jump with more impulsion. During the suspension phase, the rider will have to give more with his hands and allow the horse more freedom of the head and neck. Eventually, higher fences can also be tackled on their own. Here, as always, it is important to increase the height slowly. It makes sense to initially approach the fence from a large turn. To begin with, only individual fences should be jumped.

Jumping Higher Courses

Of course, it is not enough to be able to jump a single high fence on its own. Rather, the rider needs to practise jumping a number of high fences as a course. For this purpose, short courses with fences of differing height are set up first. After a fence of the maximum height required in a competition, a smaller fence should follow next, in order not to overtax the rider.

In time, the course will become longer and longer and more and more high fences are set up. If the rider is completely confident about jumping these courses, the trainer can introduce difficult combinations and routes. Again it is important not to overdo things, because even at a show not all fences in the competition are built to the maximum height and width. Instead the height will vary between the minimum and maximum dimension. The jumping course should start with a simple fence and slowly become more difficult.

Warming up the horse in the collecting ring before the competition is something the rider has to learn.
Photo: Hermann

UNFAMILIAR FENCES

So far, the horse has been acquainted with each fence in the riding arena in turn. As a preparation for jumping competitions at shows, the rider needs to practise jumping fences which the horse was unable to scrutinise beforehand. For this purpose, I set up a moderately easy course and only allow the horses to warm up over one or two fences in the arena. The other fences may not be jumped at this stage. Once the horses have warmed up sufficiently and are jumping at the height of the fences of the course, each rider rides the "unfamiliar" course on his own. Naturally, the riders should walk the course before jumping it. This exercise often leads to unexpected difficulties because the horses suddenly refuse in front of fences which they have always jumped before. The rider will have to ride with more impulsion and have

greater control over the horse. However he has the ideal opportunity to rehearse the behaviour at a show or on a different and unfamiliar course. The rider's ability to concentrate needs to improve, if he has to find his way through the course and at the same time jump each fence at the correct take-off line and with the correct aids, as well as taking additional note of the reactions of the horse (for example, increased backing off or shying). To make the exercise more difficult, it is ideal to be able to warm up the horse in a different place and then jump the unfamiliar course in the riding arena. Eventually, you can load your horse into a trailer or horse box and drive to a different arena to jump an unfamiliar course there.

Lead Horse

Seeing that every refusal means a small loss of trust between horse and rider, refusals should be avoided as much as they can. If an inexperienced horse has never come across a certain type of fence before and the fence is not kept as low as possible, the first attempt to jump it should be made following an experienced lead horse. Even so, it is wise to walk the horse up to the fence quietly first and show it what the fence looks like. The advantage of the lead horse is that the inexperienced horse will probably follow the other horse immediately and jump the fence at first go. It does not even get a chance to develop fear of that type of fence.

The lead horse, an experienced jumper, should be ridden towards the fence at a steady tempo and the inexperienced horse should follow two horse-lengths behind. We make use of the fact that horses are herd animals to drive the following horse over the fence. Once the inexperienced horse has jumped the fence a couple of times behind the lead horse, it will be able to jump it on its own. Then the rider takes over the function of the leader. In the course of the training, the horse should develop trust in the rider to such an extent that it will jump any unusual, unfamiliar fence when asked to do so, because it has never had any bad experiences when jumping.

Refusals

If a horse refuses, it is extremely important that it does not lose its trust in its rider. On principle, refusals should be avoided as much as possible through careful schooling. Prevention is always better than cure. Therefore the rider should only attempt tasks which he and the horse are definitely able to carry out. He needs to take his time during schooling and to have endless patience.

Despite all care, there is always a time where a horse will have a refusal. In this case, the first thing the rider must do is prevent the horse from running out on either side of the fence and drive it up to the obstacle, even if the horse will not jump. Ideally, the horse should not even learn to run out at a fence. Once it stands in front of the fence, the horse should remain there and the rider should encourage it to flex its lower jaw and lower its head. At the same time, the rider continues to apply the active aids to ride the horse forwards, in order to prevent the horse from stepping back and to make the horse step up as close to the fence as possible. Ideally, the horse should stretch its neck and inspect the fence and sniff at it. As soon as the horse demonstrates its willingness to go forward, the rider should praise the horse and approach the fence anew.

Flexing the lower jaw and lowering its head in front of the fence is a corrective measure for the horse, because at this moment it really only wants to get away from the terrifying object in front of it. By keeping the horse in front of the fence, you are demanding that it submits to the rider's will. The boredom that is created waiting in front of the fence is unbearable for the horse, so it will decide to jump instead. While you are waiting for the horse to flex its lower jaw and lower its head, you yourself should calm down and check the correct application of your aids. Any kind of aggression is completely out of order in this situation. The rider should also ask himself what the problem was in jumping this fence and try to avoid possible errors at the next approach. The horse must remain on the bit and

The rider tries to ensure that the horse does not run out to one side despite the refusal. Photo: S. Stuewer

Showing the horse a fence it has refused calmly, gives the horse the confidence to try to jump it again. Photo: C. Busch

aged to jump it there and then from a standstill. Up to a height of approximately 60 centimetres, this should present no problems. If necessary, the rider can rein the horse back a couple of strides and then push the horse into a trot and jump the fence. In my opinion, jumping a fence without having to turn the horse away from it, is the most effective corrective measure, as this will teach the horse that it has to jump the fence whatever may come and that it has no chance of avoiding this.

If the fence cannot be lowered, the rider should ride a small circle and jump the horse from this circle as soon as the horse has flexed its lower jaw and accepted the rider's aids. The rider should avoid riding too far away from the fence to gain momentum, so that the horse learns that it cannot escape the task in hand. The ideal way to go about it is to approach the fence at a trot (with fences up to a height of 1 metre), as this makes it easier to keep the horse under control and avoid arriving at the fence all wrong for the take-off.

under the rider's control until it has jumped the fence. It is possible to show a horse a fence it has refused even at a show. However the rider does not have quite so much time to do this as during a schooling session.

When a young horse has refused, the fence should be lowered completely while the rider is showing it to the horse. Then the horse should be encour-

If the horse refuses at one of the last fences in a grid or jumping lane, it should be made to jump that particular fence again on its own immediately, if possible. In a competition at a show, this however is not allowed in combinations. Of course, the horse should be ridden with extra impulsion when approaching the refused fence again, and if necessary, support the aids for the take-off with spurs and a whip. It is wrong however to smack the horse after a refusal as it will connect this nasty experience with jumping the fence, which will make it even less enthusiastic to jump again. If a horse refuses, it

If the horse has problems with walls, these should initially be jumped behind a lead horse and as low as possible.
Photo: S. Stuewer

seldom does so because it does not feel like jumping, but rather due to fear. The rider must help it overcome this fear. The horse should build up enough trust in its rider that it will jump anything the rider approaches, because it knows that nothing bad can happen. Thrashing the horse, which is usually a result of the momentary anger of the rider, will destroy this trust. Therefore the period of standing in front of the fence waiting for the horse to flex its lower jaw should also be used by the rider to calm down and start thinking again. He must never react in anger instinctively.

Difficult Types of Obstacles

During training, the rider should learn to jump a wall. To begin with, a sec- tion of a wall is placed beneath a pole as a filler. Next, the wall is integrated into the grid or jumping lane, and finally the rider learns to approach it on its own. If the horse is used to this fence, approaching a wall doesn't pre- sent a problem, as the horse will came back to the rider's aids by itself, due to the solid appearance of the fence, and it is easy to judge the correct take-off.

The triple bar causes more anxiety than it should, because it is actually a particularly easy fence to tackle, as the low front pole makes it almost impos- sible to get too close to the fence for take-off. Even if the horse jumps only 20 centimetres away from the fence, the slanting incline of the triple bar allows it to tuck its legs under without touching the first pole. This fence is

Judging the correct take-off line for a triple bar is made easier through the low front pole.
Photo: S. Stuewer

therefore particularly well suited for practising judging the take-off. The only difficulty can be whether the horse jumps far enough, if the triple bar is particularly wide.

Due to its close take-off line, the triple bar should not be included in grids and combinations. The usual distance rules do not apply to this fence. It can be set up as a first fence in front of a grid, but is not really ideal for this purpose (psychological aspect).

Water requires special accustoming. On the one hand, there are moveable rubber water jumps which are often used as a filler under a fence in modern courses, and on the other hand we have

fixed water jumps. The moveable ones are used almost exclusively under a normal upright or spread fence and therefore present no particular difficulty. Horses which are not yet used to jumping these fences should initially be jumped over a smaller version of a water jump (for example, a folded rubber fence), or right at the beginning over a rug or similar item placed underneath a small fence. The rider applies his aids with more force on the approach to the unknown fence and frames the horse between his legs and hands to prevent it from running out on either side. If necessary, a lead horse can be used.

Jumping water can be practised by initially using a rubber water ditch underneath an upright fence.
Photo: C. Busch

Jumping fixed water fences is something the rider needs to practise before competing at a show (from intermediary level onward). In the beginning, the rider should practise with his horse over a narrow ditch, maybe again using a lead horse. If necessary, the horse will have to be loaded into a trailer and transported to a place with a narrow ditch. The extra work will not have been in vain, as the rider will invariably encounter a water jump at some stage, when competing in higher-level competitions, and it is very annoying being eliminated at such a fence for lack of practice.

The approach to a water jump is taken at greater speed because the horse has to jump a width of around 6 to 7 metres (including the take-off and landing phases). The point of take-off should be as close to the water jump as possible. The important thing is to keep the horse on the bit and together at the increased speed, as it will otherwise lose the impulsion to jump.

In cases where horses tend to step into the water at the take-off, it often helps to set up a low brush fence in front of the water which marks the take-off line. If the horse touches the water either during the moment of suspension or during the landing phase, a

Fixed water jumps require an energetic approach and support of the horse. Photo: S. Stuewer

pole (up to 50 centimetres high) can be built over the water close to the back of the obstacle.

Some jumping arenas have cross-country fences such as coffins, banks and ditches. If you have the opportunity, you should practise over lower versions of these different fences at home in a field or in the outdoor arena, jumping parts of these fences on their own first (such as jumping up or down a bank) and then as a whole.

SUITABILITY OF THE HORSE

CHARACTER AND TEMPERAMENT

Only a horse which moves forwards willingly, is responsive and easy to ride and reacts well to the rider's aids is ideal for show jumping. In addition to its natural aptitude, the main thing to look for in a good show jumper is its schooling, because correct reaction to the rider's aids is not a feature horses are born with. Nowadays, lightly built horses with a high percentage of Thoroughbred blood in their veins are used for advanced show jumping. These horses are certainly suitable, but they are also very sensitive and require a correspondingly correct and sensitive treatment by the rider.

Very lazy and sluggish horses are not suitable for competitive show jumping, as it is very difficult to motivate them accordingly. It may be however that the sluggishness of the horse is due to boring, repetitive schooling and that the horse will liven up and co-operate willingly if jumping presents an exciting alternative to his dull day-to-day life. In principle, horses like these should experience as much diversity as possible and be hacked out frequently. If this makes them more lively, they can also be used as show jumpers.

A very impetuous horse is not suitable for advanced show jumping either as it does not allow the rider to control it sufficiently, and both rider and horse

This horse jumps with its forelegs well tucked in.
Photo: Ernst

use up too much energy, which they need for jumping, fighting each other. Impetuous horses need to be ridden calmly and steadily. They should walk long stretches out on hacks and in the arena. In the jumping arena, they

63

should be schooled in dressage. Harsher bits only help if the level of schooling and the willingness of the horse to accept the rider's aids improve at the same time.

HEALTH

The health of a show jumper also needs to be taken into account. A horse which has a damaged back or legs will always be in pain during jumping and therefore must not used for this purpose. Before choosing a horse for a career in top-level show jumping and spending years schooling it for this aim, the health of the animal should be checked very thoroughly. Even small changes in the bone structure or weaknesses in the legs should be examined by a veterinary surgeon. If the diagnosis is not clear, you should think long and hard whether it is worth investing vast amounts of time and money in the schooling of the horse, if there is a danger that soon it may no longer be able to jump, due to pain, or will not jump reliably, for the same reason.

ABILITY
AND TECHNIQUE

Of course, the ability of a horse, in other words, how well and how high it can jump, is a major factor in deciding to train it as a show jumper. An inexperienced person however will not find it easy to recognise how talented a very young horse is going to be. It is possible to let it jump free over fences, but you should avoid building the fences too high for this purpose, as this could put the young horse off from the start. In addition, the horse's ability will improve in the course of its training.

Therefore it is recommended to ask an expert for help, who will be able to judge the young horse, or to buy an already experienced horse, which is certainly the best option for a rider with little show jumping experience. As a rule, riders with years of experience in schooling young show jumpers, generally have a very good eye for the quality of a horse. Whether this promise will become reality in the course of the training however, also depends on the psychological make-up of the horse and the quality of the trainer and therefore remains uncertain. You should never forget this when buying a completely raw horse for show jumping.

The term "technique" refers to the leg technique of the horse, in other words its ability to fold its legs under its body over the fence. The higher fences become, the more important the technique is. This can be improved through jumping gymnastic, but should already be evident in the young horse.

JUMPING AT SHOWS*

PREPARATION

Competing at shows can begin when the rider has jumped his horse many times and without problems over a course of the height the fences will be in the competition. It is by no means sensible to go to a show and then try out which class one is able to compete in, as this will make both horse and rider lose confidence.

The first start at a show should be prepared at least six weeks in advance. Initially, in affiliated classes the novice horse can only ride in the British Novice, Discovery, Newcomers or similar events. The rider can start with a British Novice class and then, if everything has gone well, also jump the Discovery class at the same show.

The rider will have to find out at home how much time he will need to warm up his horse before the competition. Note the time you walk the horse and warm up at the rising trot, and which movements are the best to ride and for how long, to make the horse relaxed, responsive and sensitive to the rider's aids as quickly as possible. You

Horse and rider are correctly equipped for a show jumping class. Photo: Giers

should practise a variety of possibilities and then decide on the best one. The same applies for warming-up over fences.

In addition, the rider should become acquainted with the requirements of the competition in good time. You need to know how high and wide the maximum dimensions of the fences are, which speed is demanded in this particular class (for example 350 metres per minute). The rules (for compet-

---

Note: in the original German edition of this book the author talks exclusively about affiliated show jumping classes, as unaffiliated classes and small locally organised shows are prohibited in Germany. The text has been amended accordingly to apply mainly to affiliated show jumping in England, which is regulated by the British Show Jumping Association (BSJA). The general recommendations apply whatever show the rider enters for.

itions in England) are set out in the Year Book of the British Show Jumping Association (BSJA). The speed as well as the height of the fences need to be practised. Take care however not to overdo things and sour the horse. Jumping courses and gymnastic jumping always need to be done alternately, which is another reason for the early start of the special preparation time.

The rider needs to know which bits and other equipment he is allowed to use according to the BSJA rules, as it is extremely annoying for the rider to be disqualified for having the wrong equipment. Normally horses can be ridden in loose-ring and egg-butt snaffle, as well as kimberwick and pelham and sometimes Dutch gag. Make sure however to use the bits in their correct fashion (pelham with connecting straps and one pair of reins). Running martingales, tendon boots and over-reach boots are allowed in all classes and should be used to protect the horse's legs (at home as well as in competitions).

The type of class must be clarified as well. The rider needs to know exactly how many faults he will incur when dropping a pole, for having a refusal or losing the way. Unfortunately most riders are not always sufficiently informed. Quite apart from the fact that they will not achieve the optimum result in the appropriate class, they are also unable to lodge an appeal in case the judges got it wrong. It does not happen very often but it does occur and is annoying.

Each show jumping class has its own rules. There are classes judged on style (not usual in England), clear round jumping with or without jump-off (fastest time and least faults wins), hurry scurries, maximum points classes and many more. In addition, different judging procedures can be used. Therefore you have to know what the emphasis of the class is (time, style, points, etc.) in order to be able to plan your ride. The show schedule will tell you exactly which rules of the BSJA apply in each class.

SHOEING

The horse's shoes should be checked one week in advance of the show. If the horse was last shod six or more weeks ago, it needs new shoes. The danger of losing a shoe is much higher at a show than at home.

In jumping classes it is often necessary to use studs to stop the horse from slipping. The studs however must not be put in until immediately before warming-up for the class, and should be removed after jumping the course, in order to prevent injuries. During transportation in particular studs should be removed, as the risk is great that the horse may kick itself. Injuries to the coronet band are difficult to treat and need a long time to heal. No studs are needed in the indoor or outdoor arena. In some countries the farrier will fix small pins to the shoes which are sufficient for these surfaces.

The type of ground determines the type of stud to use. In most cases small, rounded jumping studs are sufficient to stop the horse from slipping on the grass. Long pointed studs should only be used in extremely boggy and heavy going. In such cases the rider should deliberate whether to

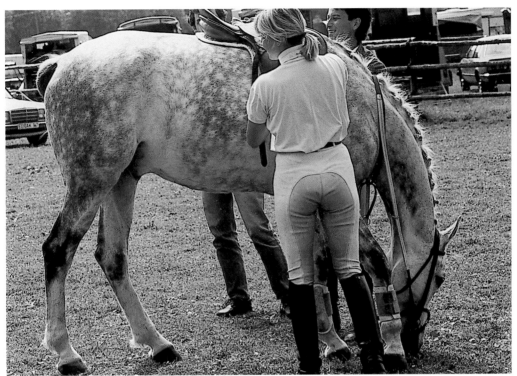

Preparations at a show should be done calmly and in plenty of time. Haste and stress knock the confidence of horse and rider.
Photo: Hermann

withdraw from the class altogether if the going is too bad, as this can endanger the health of the horse. In addition, the horse can be put off jumping, if it slips during the take-off and landing phase. Most horses then become fearful and will refuse to jump. In my opinion it is not worth taking this risk for a (possible) placing in the class. For jumping classes which are run on a sand arena in bad weather, small round or square jumping studs are sufficient.

The danger of slipping is also present on a dry grass surface. Many riders don't take this into account. If you are not sure whether the horse will slip, you can ride turns in the warming-up ring and test whether the ground is safe.

Screwing in the studs presents no problems as long as the stud holes have been kept clean and are filled in with cotton wool dipped in hoof oil, stud sleepers, or a similar material as soon as the studs are removed to prevent any dirt from getting in. Then the cotton wool will only have to be removed before screwing in the stud. Do not over-tighten the studs as this could pull the shoe awry.

WARMING-UP

You should plan the arrival at the showground with plenty of time in hand, so that you have time to take a look around, get your horse ready and warm it up before the class. If you arrive at the last minute and have to get your horse ready in a hurry, it is very unlikely that you will ride a good round.

After arriving at the showground the first thing to do is to see to the horse

During jumping the rider remains concentrated and retains the overview over the course.
Photo: S. Stuewer

and then go to the secretary's tent, either to enter the class, or if you sent in your entry in advance, to fetch your number and confirm your presence and that you are going to jump. Then you should put your number down for the class and find out how long it will take until you are due in the arena. Then look at the course and walk it, if possible (you may have to do this after warming up your horse). For safety's sake you should add twenty minutes to the warming-up time to allow for possible unforeseen delays (for example, unloading the horse may take longer, the horse is nervous, or other riders don't turn up). If everything goes as planned, this extra time can then be bridged by riding the horse around at a walk.

Walking the Course

The rider should first walk the course with an experienced rider, who can advise and give tips. Riders may only enter the arena after it has been cleared by the judges (bell or announcement). Riders have to walk the course in correct clothing, in other words boots, breeches or jodhpurs, riding jacket, hat, and whip (the latter two can be carried in one hand).

First, the rider should focus on the start line, in order not to cross it before the bell rings for the rider to start jumping the course, and not to forget it after the bell has rung. You should cross the line at an ideal angle to approach the first fence.

Then every fence of the course is inspected, walking the route you intend to take with your horse between the fences. Make sure to memorise the points where you have to turn and how large you want to ride each turn. Observe each new fence from a distance first and then close up. Also check on the condition of the ground on the approach to the fences and behind them. Extremely heavy going requires a more energetic approach. In addition, you should check whether the approach to the fence is level, uphill, or downhill. Memorise all these things.

You have to walk the distances in combinations and related distances and decide how to ride them. As a rule this will not present a problem in novice classes with a horse with a normal stride, as each horse has enough ability to compensate for distances which are not quite right. When jumping at an advanced level, you will have to measure the distance precisely and decide how to ride a combination or a related distance. Also have a look at the finish line so that you can cross it in the shortest possible time and not forget it altogether.

In a jumping class with a jump-off, you should also have a good look at the jump-off course, as you will not have time to do this later, if you do get into the jump-off. You will find the sequence of the jump-off course on the course plan which is posted at the entrance to the arena and in the secretary's tent. Some fences may be removed from the original course for the jump-off, as they could be in the way (in this case it is possible that only the second fence of a combination is part of the jump-off course). If necessary, you can always ask the course clerk which fences will be used in the jump-off.

Preparation of the Horse

If the horse is not used to going to shows, it should be led around near the jumping arena and warming-up area to accustom it to the atmosphere (lead the horse on the bridle).

A further possibility to prepare high-spirited horses is to lunge it. This will calm it down and give it a chance to become acquainted with the new environment. It is then easier for the rider to ride the horse which has been lunged and there is no danger of a tussle between horse and rider.

The rider should try to create a relaxed atmosphere for his horse in the warming-up area.
Photo: Hermann

Then the horse is prepared for riding and ridden on a long rein either in the warming-up area or around the place until it has become accustomed to the situation and has had a good look around. If the rider starts working the horse before this, the horse will not concentrate on the rider, causing problems. This should be avoided if possible.

The horse is warmed up at a trot and canter, until he is as responsive to the aids and collected and on the bit as he normally is at home. Depending on the horse's predisposition, the rider should perform movements and transitions to ensure that the horse is relaxed and responsive to an optimum degree. Getting the horse to respond willingly to the rider's aids and concentrate on the rider on the bit and collectedly, is more important than the warming-up jump-

ing in the warming-up arena. Basically, jumping at this stage is predominantly important for the rider, so that he can concentrate on the task ahead. Three to four practice jumps would be perfectly sufficient for the horse to prepare for the jumping course (that is in the normal case; there are of course horses who form the exception). Don't forget to tighten the girth in the general excitement. The best thing to do is to make a check list before going to a show of all things that need to be done in the correct chronological order, and ask an assistant to cross out each item on the list so that nothing gets forgotten.

Then, the rider should start jumping with the help of an assistant. First of all the practice fences should all be approached at the trot. For this purpose, the fences are raised slowly up to a height of 1 metre. These fences from the trot are important to give both the horse and the rider a feeling of security and confidence. The horse should lose its fear of the unknown environment by doing simple exercises it is used to from its schooling at home.

Then the jumps should be approached at the canter. It is imperative that the rider concentrates on judging the take-off. Under competition conditions this is more difficult as one gets distracted more easily. Also, the surface could be different and the horse may feel unfamiliar due to the tension of being in a strange place. All these difficulties should be brought under control by jumping low fences, so as to get confidence. That is the purpose of warming up.

It is sensible to jump a few fences at the maximum height of the competition, as horse and rider have to get used to the different take-off distance of the higher fences. Afterwards however the rider should go back to lower fences. Jumping fences which are too high is not recommended as this will have the opposite of the desired effect, namely loss of confidence. Therefore, the rider should avoid jumping fences which are higher than those of the competition. It is important not to overdo the number of jumps in the warming-up phase. As a rule, ten to fifteen jumps are enough. Try not to ask for more warming-up jumps than you would at home, because the danger of making the horse feel insecure through jumps that go wrong increases with the number of fences jumped. It is a better idea to fully concentrate on taking one fence every now and then and to correct the faults made. The rider should get a feeling of how a good jump feels like and

A good assistant is worth his or her weight in gold. Photo: Jahraus

try to recreate this situation time and time again. Constant hectic jumping will have exactly the opposite effect and horse and rider will become distracted and nervous and will enter the show jumping arena with their nerves in tatters. During the pauses between jumping you should ride your horse at a walk on a loose rein to reduce stress and tension levels. You should take deep breaths and imagine how you are going to jump each fence of the

While waiting for one's turn to jump, the rider should maintain the concentration. Photo: Hermann

course correctly. This is also a good opportunity to recount the course in your head, with all its details. During this time, your horse will also relax and be able to perform its task much better.

If possible, you should watch one or two other riders before your turn comes. It is best to select riders who have already created a good impression in the warming-up area, or where you know that they will ride a competent round with their horse. Watching a bad round usually creates a negative basic attitude. Our subconscious can trick us here and suggest that we will have the same problems that we have just observed. You should not let this feeling of insecurity arise. Keep on telling yourself that you will be able to

tackle the task in hand well, as you and your horse have practised sufficiently at home and that you will be easily be able to fulfil all the set tasks.

Starting the Class as First Rider

If you are the first rider to ride the course, you will have to reorganise your warming-up session. In this case, you need to warm up your horse before the class starts and then walk the course. In addition to the planned warming-up phase, you need to plan in an extra fifteen minutes, during which you walk the course. You will have to organise to have an assistant ready beforehand, who will lead or ride your horse at a walk in the meantime. You can take your time walking the course, if your horse is already sufficiently warmed up. Before the start of walking the course stay near the entrance as much as possible in order to be able to enter the arena as soon as you are permitted. Once you have finished, prepare the horse for the task ahead again for a few minutes, jump another fence to focus the horse on jumping and then ride to the entrance. If you are unable to jump another fence, making the horse rein back a few strides will have to suffice to refocus its concentration. For many riders the idea of having to go first is an unpleasant thought. This is completely unnecessary however because it can actually have its advantages. The ground in front of the fences, for example, is still in an optimum condition for your horse. In addition, you can tackle the task in hand without a care in the world and fulfil it just as you have schooled successfully so often at home, without having observed other riders, which can make you lose confidence. Often, this is better than last minute advice on how to jump the course, because other riders have just had problems at certain fences. You should never let anybody else convince you that you may face problems. You have already successfully jumped a course of the same height, and you can do so again.

Jumping the Course

Enter the arena at a trot and ride a small circle through the course in the direction of the judges. You should have memorised the route you take upon entering the arena when walking the course. Then stop the horse and bow to the judges. In the past, men took of their helmets and women dropped the right arm and nodded their head. With riding helmets now all having a three-point harness, men greet the judges in the same way as women do. The rider greets the judges and thereby is subject to their judging as the recognised experts under the BSJA rules.

If your horse is very nervous, you may also greet the judges at a walk. However, you should practise slowing the horse to a halt. Next, take up your reins and start trotting. Then change to the jumping seat and drive the horse into a canter towards the first fence. You have to wait however for the judges to ring the bell and clear you for start-off. If you cross the start line before the bell goes, you will be disqualified. Normally, the bell rings as soon as the rider has greeted the judges. Sometimes however, if a previously knocked down fence has not been resurrected yet, or if the course helpers have not reached their allocated positions, the starter bell will be delayed. In the meantime you have the opportunity to ride your horse around the course and to accustom it to the atmosphere.

If you aren't sure whether the start signal has been given and you did not hear it, do not under any circumstances simply start the course, but rather ride to the judges' box and ask them whether the bell has rung. There is no need to get yourself into a panic if the starter's bell has gone. You have 60 seconds to get ready and cross the start line. You should however start without delay in order not to cause the entire timetable of the show, which is probably very tight, to collapse.

Once you have crossed the start line your ride will be judged. Small circles

Horse and rider enter the arena calmly and ride towards the judges' box.
Photo: Hermann

and turns in front of the start line do not count. Increase your speed when crossing the start line and collect your horse together. Inexperienced show jumping riders often start riding the course without the necessary impulsion, because they feel weak in the knees or have butterflies in their stomach. This lack of determination will transfer itself to the horse and it may hesitate at the first fence. You therefore have to muster all your power and drive the horse towards the first fence with vigorous aids.

As the first fence is always slightly lower and more inviting, it doesn't necessarily matter if you don't get the stride right. Once the rider has jumped the first fence, one difficult hurdle has been overcome. The rider can them tackle the next fence with the same vigour.

It is important to remember always to put your horse on the bit between the fences and collect it again to ensure that the horse does not start going flat, or you will be unable to place it at the correct take-off for the fence.

After every fence, the sometimes relatively short distance to the next fence needs to be used to ride the horse

ie Delve

Because he has practised for this, the rider is not disturbed by the spectators when approaching a fence.
Photo: S. Stuewer

back onto the bit with vigorous for-ward-driving aids. You always have to know where to go next, and you need to concentrate solely on jumping the next fence and the route to take after that fence. Do not let yourself be distracted.

Most importantly you should not allow yourself to become irritated by falling poles. There is no time in a show jumping round for error analysis. Simply forget the fault and its effect on your result or a possible placing and make every effort to jump the rest of the course as well as possible. You also

need to be aware of the danger of the final fence. If everything so far has gone well, the temptation to "stop riding" now is great. Force yourself to ride the last fence with the same con-centration as the others and then canter through the finish line by the shortest route possible.

After that you can relax, praise your horse, slow it down to a trot and exit the arena reasonably speedily.

In schooling sessions, it is important to continue to practise jumping small fences at the trot or canter in order to give the horse confidence and to avoid refusals. Photo: A. Busch

FAULT ANALYSIS AND CORRECTIVE MEASURES

Knocking down poles

In your first shows, you should simply ignore fallen poles. If your horse is jumping fences at this height faultlessly at home, the problem is most likely nervousness at the show. If the horse is still inexperienced, it is certainly possible that it will be distracted by the many impressions and noises at a show, and therefore jumps the fences with insufficient concentration. You should calmly take it up and ride it back on the bit after the landing and encourage it to concentrate through applying the right aids. After a few shows, the nervousness will disappear and in time the horse will produce the same performance as it does at home.

Refusals

Refusals incurred at a show need to be analysed in depth, as this can quickly become a bad habit which will make successful show jumping impossible. The rider should clarify with his trainer whether the refusal was caused by the rider's aids, by extreme nervousness or fear on the part of the horse, by fences which were too high or too unfamiliar, or was due to lack of schooling. It is important that the rider applies the correct aids in the event of a refusal. At first he should influence his horse with the aids in such a way that the horse cannot run out on either side of the fence. For this purpose the horse is framed more strongly between hands and legs and ridden forwards with plenty of impulsion. Very often that is all that is needed to eliminate this bad habit. If the horse stops, it should stop directly in front of the fence and not run out on either side. As the chances of being placed in a competition fly out of the window anyway once the horse has refused, you can now let the horse stand calmly in front of the fence for a moment (showing a horse a fence it has refused is permitted), calm it down if necessary and then approach the jump again within 60 seconds from as short distance as possible, using stronger back and leg aids and maybe the whip which is used at the shoulder of the horse before the moment of take-off, and usually jump the fence at the second attempt.

If the horse has run out to one side, you should ride it back to the fence, show him this fence from close up, and then approach it again. You will have no chance of getting placed anyhow, so it is better to take your time to give your horse more confidence. If the horse refuses again, you should praise the horse after a successful corrective jump and leave the course. In this case, all you have to do is raise your hand to the judges. If refusals become a grave matter, there is no point in risking a third refusal over the rest of the course. Instead, the rider should practise jumping the horse on unfamiliar schooling courses where he can correct the refusals in his own good time, or compete the horse in a more novice event until it jumps the course with confidence.

If your horse refuses the same fence twice, you should consider whether the fence is too high or too difficult for the horse in some other way. If this is the case, the sensible thing to do is choose an easier fence (for example the first fence) as a correction jump, instead of getting three refusals at the same fence. By jumping a different fence, preferab-

ly a simple upright which the horse has already jumped, you resign from the competition and need to leave the course after the corrective jump. A further corrective jump is not permitted.

If your horse has refused a third time, the bell will ring and you are eliminated. You do have the choice however to jump any fence (with the exception of a combination) as a corrective jump. Again, choose one of the easy fences.

Refusals in a Combination
If your horse refuses in a combination, all fences of that combination (including the ones already jumped) need to be jumped again. All faults which occur at this second attempt are added to the end result, even if you went clear over parts of the combination at the first attempt. You need to memorise which fences are combinations during the walking of the course in order to know exactly what to do in the event of a refusal. Of course you are allowed to show your horse the fence it has refused before continuing.

However you need to make sure that two fences which follow each other directly, really are a combination rather than a related distance. Double and treble combinations have a distance between fences of one stride (7 metres) or two strides (10.5 metres). Related distances on the other hand have a distance between fences of three strides (14 metres) or four strides (17.5 metres). You will have to work out the number of strides when walking the course and take note of the numbers at each fence. Combinations have the same number, but are marked A, B and C. Related distances have sequential numbers.

In the case of unusual fences, the rider should reinforce his aids and contact with the horse's mouth during the approach.
Photo: Ernst

If the horse refuses at the first fence of the combination, it will have scared itself so thoroughly at the sight of the following fences that it refuses for safety's sake. If you stand directly in front of the combination when walking the course, you can see that the sequence of jumps looks very threatening to the horse and that it cannot see on the approach whether it has sufficient space between the fences to land. This can be rectified by riding through the individual fences of the combination when entering the arena. If the horse has already refused, you should show the first fence to the horse so it can also see the following fences a bit better. In addition, you should remember to set up massive combinations with fillers, wings and a lot of poles at home and practise these with the horse. The horse has to learn that it can rely on the rider, if asked to perform such a task. It is imperative that the horse gains experience in jumping combinations.

If the horse refuses at the second or third fence of a combination, the fault is usually a wrong take-off. Either the rider misjudged the first fence and the wrong distance is carried through to the following obstacles, or the distances in the combinations do not match the stride of the horse. Here, it would be sensible to ask yourself during the time that you are showing the fence to the horse or are turning back for a second attempt, where the error lies. If you have come too close you need to increase the speed slightly; if you jumped too wide, you need to slow down the tempo and collect the horse more. It is then important for the rider to concentrate fully on approaching the fence and judge the take-off correctly. Under no circumstances should the rider stand up too high over the fence and tip forward, as the horse will be unable to approach the following fence immediately and with the necessary impulsion. If the take-off distances to the second or third fence did not fit because the horse hesitated, for example, the rider needs to react with determination. Always remember that you have no problems at home jumping combinations; take a deep breath and jump the combination at the next attempt.

Refusals in a closed combination

The closed combination is a special type of fence. Here, the rider cannot get out for a second approach between two parts of the combination. In most cases closed combinations are natural cross-country fences such as a bank or a coffin where the placing of the fence does not allow the horse to leave the combination any way but over a fence. In this case, the next fence must be jumped without leaving the combination. The difficulty here is of course the extremely short approach to the second or third element of the combination. All you can do is ride a small circle and approach the fence with one or two strides. If the fence is not too high the rider should jump it from the trot as this makes judging the correct take-off line easier. Jumping fences with only a minimum approach distance is something the rider should practise at home. During a schooling session fences of normal height are jumped from the trot (the height of the fences should be increased slowly).

In the beginning you should place a take-off pole in front of the fence to hit

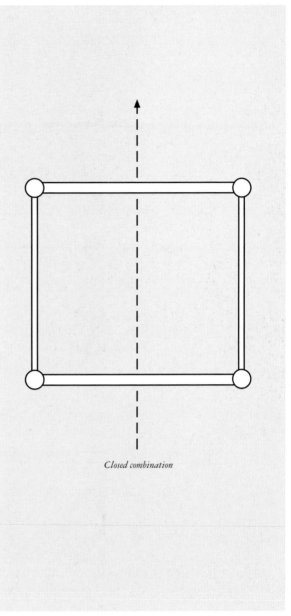

Closed combination

Closed combination in the jumping course plan.

the ideal take-off line. Later, this pole is removed. Approaching a fence from a loop is another exercise to practise. For this purpose you should put up a fence in a position where the horse has to jump it coming out of a loop in the corner. The diameter of the loop should be reduced to eight to ten metres.

To recognise a closed combination, the rider needs to have a look at the jumping course plan. In the case of closed combinations, the fences of the combination are framed, open combinations are drawn as open. In the case of a closed combination the rider needs to have a very good look to see how he should react in the event of a refusal.

Corrective Measures in the Warming-Up Area

Judges and organisers don't like to see a rider use corrective measures in the warming-up area after jumping a course, which is understandable because it is often misunderstood and sometimes comes close to cruelty towards the horse. Quite apart from that, it disrupts the course of the competition, if riders who have already jumped go back to the warming-up area. If you have been eliminated however and your horse also refused the correction fence, you should go back to the warming-up area and jump one simple fence. It is enough to jump a small fence from the trot. Afterwards the horse should be praised and walked around until it has dried off. As in a schooling session, the horse always needs to end the session with a well performed task. Sometimes the requirements have to be lowered extremely in order to achieve a positive result. It does not matter to the horse how high or wide the correction fence is. The important thing is that it jumps the fence without a problem and regains its confidence.

To punish the horse in the warming-up area for its behaviour on the course is completely useless, as the horse cannot make the connection between the two. All you can ask it to do is carry out a simple task correctly

Nervousness

Nervousness at the first show is often the reason for faults which the horse would not make at home. In this case the rider needs to work on his basic attitude. It is completely normal to initially have butterflies in one's stomach. This should not be overdone however and the rider should not convince himself that everything will go wrong. In this case, the rider's subconscious will be only too happy to oblige. You must tell yourself over and over again that you can fulfil the tasks set out. You have thoroughly schooled your horse at home and will achieve a good result, taking into account slight mistakes due to the initial nervousness. Always concentrate on the task in hand and imagine how you will ride the jumping course at the show, or how you have jumped the last successful course at home, how things are going to work out and how you will approach each fence at the correct distance and jump it faultlessly

TYPES OF SHOW JUMPING CLASS

CLASSES JUDGED ON STYLE

Classes judged on style are very rare in England but are common in Germany, where they are usually provided in novice classes. The reason for this is that the judges check the seat and the rider's aids in particular and correct these if possible so that the rider is better prepared for higher jumping classes.

In show jumping classes judged on style, the correct aids over the fence are judged in particular.
Photo: Jahraus

Classes for juniors and young riders are almost always judged on style in Germany. The style of the rider is judged but this should not mean that you enter with a less well schooled horse, but continue to school it in dressage to improve its acceptance of the rider's aids. An unresponsive horse will not achieve a good mark for the style of the rider over a fence.

The forward seat and the jumping seat of the rider are judged primarily over the fence. The rumour that good results can only be achieved if the rider stays in the forward seat continuously, with his seat well above the saddle, is not true. On the contrary, the judges look for a combination of different forms of the forward seat and the jumping seat. The rider is expected to relieve his horse's back over the entire course but needs to sit down deeper in order to approach the fences correctly and to

If the legs slip back at the moment of suspension over the fence, this will count against a good mark in classes judged on style.
Photo: S. Stuewer

During the moment of suspension, the rider must relieve the horse's back, adopting the jumping seat. This is also judged in this type of jumping class. The judges want to see the particular elasticity in the hip and shoulders of the rider following his horse's movement and like to see a straight back. The rider should stay with his horse the entire time and should not disturb it or fall heavily into the saddle. Judging the correct take-off line of the fence is an important factor of course, because only a properly judged jump can be ridden in optimum style.

The connection between the rider's hands and the mouth of the horse should not mean that the horse canters continuously with a flexed poll and low head carriage, as horses tend to canter on the forehand, if they are ridden with too much collection of the reins and not enough impulsion of the legs and are therefore forced to jump with too much weight on the forehand. The horse should be on the bit, responsive to the rider's aids and cantering "uphill". The line of the nose of the horse does not have to be vertical, as long as the horse uses its back actively.

During the moment of suspension, the rider should give enough rein that the horse is able to balance itself optimally with a stretched neck. The rider's fists remain closed and the elbows should not stick out to both sides. Over the fence the rider needs to follow the stretching of the horse's neck, while maintaining gentle contact with its mouth. During the landing phase, he should take up the connection to the horse's mouth without jerking on the reins.

maintain the balance of horse and rider when riding turns. This requires the adoption of the forward seat, which allows a more or less deep seat in the saddle with the rider's upper body leaning forward, depending on the responsiveness and schooling level of the horse. How deep the rider should sit and take his upper body back depends on the situation. The ideal way is to ride in the forward seat, and gently lower oneself into the saddle on the approach to a fence, without adopting the dressage seat. The rider's stirrups must not be too long as this would make the forward seat impossible.

The rider's legs should always lie against the horse's body and must not slip back when the horse takes off. The rider's weight is distributed in the stirrups via his legs. His heels should flex deeply if the ankles are relaxed. The rider's toes are pointed slightly outward, but the spurs must not be in constant contact with the horse.

The tempo should be forward-going but the horse should not rush, and most importantly the pace must be steady. Slowing down the horse significantly in front of the fence and then speeding up after the landing phase should be avoided at all costs. Instead the horse should canter rhythmically with a steady tempo. Shortening and lengthening the stride should not influence the rhythm but only ensure that the horse gains or loses ground.

Another criterion in jumping classes judged on style, is the correctness of the route between and approach to the fences, and the maintenance of ideal lines. This requires foresight on the part of the rider as well as correct leg aids in order to prevent the horse from drifting or cantering crookedly. All fences should be approached in the centre. The lines between the fences can be a bit more generous than in timed jumping classes, but the rider should avoid overly extravagant turns. This could also lead to the horse exceeding the time limit and thereby having points deducted from the score. In jumping classes judged on style with standard requirements, the route is determined in advance and the rider can practise the respective course at home.

In show jumping classes judged on style, the harmonious overall impression of horse and rider over a smoothly ridden course are vital. Photo: Jahraus

During training the horse needs to learn to jump faultlessly and in good style even at a faster speed. Photo: Ernst

TIMED SHOW JUMPING AND JUMP-OFF

Riding without faults

There is a wide variety of show jumping classes judged on faults and time. The BSJA Yearbook lists these. It is important that the rider knows which rules apply to his class in order to ride accordingly. In jumping classes judged on faults and time the most important thing is to jump the course without a fault. In addition, the time required for this is recorded and the rider with the least number of faults and the fastest time wins. Therefore, riders usually try to jump the course as fast as possible. This however brings the danger that the fences are no longer approached correctly, that the horse jumps flat, as it is no longer ridden on the bit, or that the shortened routes lead to jump-

Out hunting the horse needs to be able to jump at high speed.
Photo: S. Stuewer

ing faults. One jumping fault (that means four points if at least one pole has been dislodged) puts the rider behind all those clear rounds which were ridden at lesser speed. Jumping judged purely on time at an advanced level is the exception, of course.

Jumping Fences at Greater Speed

The rider must find the happy medium between fast and faultless jumping. He will need to school his horse for this especially. A particularly fast ride is a mixture of tight turns at a shortened canter and increased speed on straight routes. To begin with, the rider needs to practise jumping fences at higher speed. Judging the correct take-off line is more difficult at high speed, because the strides become longer and the approach to the fence is that much faster.

To begin with, the rider should jump a cross-pole or a cavaletti at high speed without bothering about judging the take-off. The horse needs to learn to pull towards the fence and to find his jumping rhythm at the faster tempo. The temperament of the horse needs to be taken into account here. Excitable horses can get out of control through the increased tempo and cannot be ridden towards the fences in an ideal manner. In this case the rider needs to increase the speed very carefully and make the horse take fences from the trot in between.

Once the horse and rider have become accustomed to the higher speed, it is time to learn to judge the correct take-off line. The increased length of the individual strides should be compensated for by pushing the horse forward, i.e., by increasing the length of the stride rather than holding the horse back. With a bit of practice the rider will become used to the new rhythm and can then judge the take-off at an increased tempo. Now the fence is made higher and other fences added bit by bit, until horse and rider can jump an entire course at higher speed.

It is very important to keep the horse together despite the lengthened stride. In between the fences, the rider needs to continuously correct the posture of the horse, by means of half-halts. The connection to the horse's mouth is slightly stronger than at a slower speed. Lengthening the reins is the usual reason for a refusal when jumping at high speed, as the horse has too little contact to the rider's hands and canters on the forehand.

Tight Corners

The rider needs to be able to reduce the high tempo drastically at any time, so that the horse can take corners as tightly as possible. Horses which canter forward at high speed throughout but cannot be slowed down will always be slower in the end result than horses which can be collected before each turn and which can "turn on a sixpence". A good preparation is the practice of making changes of tempo, which also strengthens the muscles of the horse and prepares it perfectly for jumping at high speed.

For timed show jumping, it is important that the horse does not lose impulsion in a tight corner. Therefore the hindquarters must be engaged to an optimum degree. To practise this, the rider slows the horse down from a gallop to a collected canter, turns it immediately as tightly as possible and then speeds up again out of the corner. This kind of schooling should be alternated with calm exercises, to ensure that the nerves and legs of the horse are not overtaxed. Cantering small circles and half-turns on the haunches supports these schooling exercises. Finally, the rider also practises turning immediately after landing. He should turn the horse alternately to the right and to the left onto a tight circle immediately on landing, so that he can ride away from the fence in the opposite direction.

Naturally, only individual fences can be approached and jumped out of a turn. In combinations, the last two to three strides at the canter need to be straight in order to be able to ride straight at the second fence after jumping the first. If the horse jumps a combination from a turn, the distance to the following fence will no longer be correct, due to the slanted approach. This can lead to a refusal or a jumping fault.

Approaching a Fence at an Angle

In order to become extremely fast, it is often necessary in a jump-off or timed jumping class to approach a fence at an angle and not straight, as the direct route saves time. This is called jump-

Approaching a fence at a slant can save a lot of time in timed show jumping classes. Photo: Beyrer

ing at an angle, because the approach to the jump is at an angle. Practising approaches at an angle should be done over a low fence as usual. To begin with, the angle should not be too acute and the obstacle should be framed by wings or poles in order to prevent the horse from running out on the side of the fence. Once the horse jumps with confidence, it is just a matter of practice to sharpen the angle up to 45 degrees. It is important that the horse remains responsive to the aids.

Judging the take-off line from an angle however is difficult for both horse and rider as there is no clear ground line with which to orientate oneself. The optimum point of take-off is slightly further away from the fence,

and can be marked in the sand or with a trotting pole for practising purposes. Approaching a fence at an angle is particularly suitable for uprights. Oxers on the other hand become too wide due to the greater take-off distance in front of the fence, and this could lead the horse to refuse.

Walking the Course and Overview

Walking the course is of extreme importance for timed show jumping classes. Here you have to decide which route to take, where you can cut corners and which alternatives you have, should things not always go according to plan on the course. In order to get an eye for the best route to take over a course as fast as possible, and for which

Free jumping is ideal to develop the ability of the horse to judge the take-off line and to react fast. Photo: S. Stuewer

turns and angles are possible, the rider needs to practise judging the best routes in advance at home. You should walk a course with your trainer and consider where you can cut corners or increase speed. Initially your ideas of what is possible from the ground will diverge strongly from what you can actually do once you are on the horse. That is why you have to estimate routes correctly, because there is nothing as unpleasant as finding out on the course that you cannot ride the planned route and that you have to reorganise yourself in a hurry. In order to be able to ride a course at the fastest possible speed, the rider's overview is of predominant importance. A rider who knows exactly which fence comes next and which one after that, and where he has to ride a tight turn or increase speed, and so on, will be much faster than a rider who has to think after the landing where to go next. Therefore the rider's memory needs to be kept fit during schooling sessions with the aid of difficult courses.

The horse rounds its back with its neck low in a perfectly shaped bascule. Photo: C. Busch

SCHOOLING OF THE HORSE

JUMPING TRAINING

Schooling the horse to improve its manner of jumping fences is just as important as schooling the rider. After all, the horse is an athlete and needs to train its muscles and its sequence of motion for the specific tasks which are demanded of it. This is particularly true in the case of young horses which are just starting their career as show jumpers. If the schooling at home has been thorough, the horse will have no problems performing his tasks at shows and later fulfilling the demands of advanced show jumping.

BASCULE

Bascule is the term used for the stretching and rounding over a fence of the horse's back from the withers. A good bascule can be recognised by the rounded topline of the horse, the neck which is stretched forwards and downward over the jump, the relaxed swinging tail and the contented look with pricked ears of the horse. The better a horse rounds its back, the higher it can jump and clear the fence without a fault. Pushing the back muscles down against the natural movement leads to pain in the horse and is caused primarily by riders' hands which are too heavy over the fence. In this case, the horse's back remains straight. The horse lays back its ears, does not fold its legs, and raises its neck, during the moment of suspension over the fence.

Propulsion and jumping manner help the horse clear fences without incurring faults. Photo: Hölscher

Grids are the best method to teach the horse to bascule over fences. Inviting-looking wide oxers should be set up in grids (making sure that the distances are not too great). The rider needs to give well with his hands and relieve the horse's back. The height and width of the fences is increased bit by bit.

In order to encourage the horse to look down over the fence, and thereby improve the rounding of its back muscles, a rug or similar item can be placed beneath the fence. When approaching independent fences, the rider needs to take special note of the correct take-off line and stay with the horse's movement. If the rider still finds this difficult, he will have to jump a horse which does not use its back over a fence primarily over gymnastic jumping lanes and over fences with a take-off pole.

TAKE-OFF MOMENTUM AND STYLE

The manner in which the horse folds its legs and the propulsion of its hindquarters are important criteria for a faultless clearance of fences. The horse should push itself off the ground with momentum and fold its front and hind legs well underneath its body. It needs to react as quickly as possible and never let its legs hang down. In order to improve the horse's style, it is recommended to practise in-outs, gymnastic grids from the trot and jumping lanes with upright fences from the canter, varying the distances between the fences. The horse has to develop its ability to react fast. For this purpose it is possible to shorten a correct distance between two fences for a second approach and ride at the fence at the same tempo as before, so that the horse lands slightly nearer to the second fence and must tuck in its front legs quickly and as much as possible in order not to incurr a fault. If it does touch the pole, this can be seen as a form of corrective measure, as sensitive horses will only make that mistake once. In my opinion, nothing can be gained by the method of rapping, whereby the trainer tries to scare the horse or cause it pain to such an extent that it will fold its legs better in future or jump higher. This will only cause the horse to experience fear and will increase the probability of subsequent refusals, rather than improve its style. Improving the horse's style over fences can only be achieved through intelligent jumping gymnastics.

The hind legs of the horse should be pulled back and up from the hip joint downward. To exercise the hind legs in particular, the horse should be schooled over wide oxers with differing distances in grids and jumping lanes. The horse's propulsion over a jump can be improved in particular by jumping fences from the trot, as the horse does not have the chance to jump through the impulsion of the canter stride but has to push itself off the ground powerfully and energetically from a calm tempo.

ABILITY TO JUDGE THE TAKE-OFF AND RESPONSIVENESS

The ability of the horse to judge the take-off is improved by slowly removing take-off poles, or by free jumping. During schooling sessions, the horse should always be encouraged to find its own take-off distance over low fences, with no influence on the rider's part. Make sure however that the demands are not too great. At the end of the schooling period, the horse should be able to jump a single pole at a fence and clear it faultlessly. Responsiveness and the ability to react fast are encouraged by alternating different fences and distances. Under no circumstances should the horse be allowed to become bored during jumping practice, as it will then become careless and make errors. The more varied the training session is, the better prepared the horse will be for unfamiliar courses at the showground.

SELF-CONFIDENCE

The confidence of the horse in its own ability needs to be built up steadily in the course of its training, by increasing the height of the fences with correct distances. At the beginning of its show jumping career, the horse has no idea how high it can jump. The rider needs to take it carefully and patiently to the limits of its capabilities. For this purpose, wide oxers (also called parallel oxers where the front and back pole are the same height) are of good use. They teach the horse to "let itself go and fly" when approaching them in a grid or jumping lane. The dimensions have to be increased step by step and the rider needs to ensure that the horse always jumps smaller fences which boost its confidence in between. The rider needs to ride the horse forwards powerfully on approach to the fence so that the horse is able to push off with plenty of impulsion and jump a great width.

MENTAL TRAINING

Other sporting activities such as skiing, tennis or golf would be unthinkable without the inclusion of mental training. Here, top experts are engaged as mental trainers for huge sums in order to give the athletes the correct attitude and motivation, without which it is impossible to win any competition. In this respect, riding is lagging behind. Only the technical process is practised; the mental state of the rider is not taken into account. This should be changed as soon as possible. There are several possibilities to implement mental training. For one, the competitive situation can be simulated and the rider can be taught the correct attitude and motivation, for another, kinetic processes which are not reproduced correctly due to mental blockages can be improved through mental training.

RELAXATION

If you want to influence your subconscious and give it instructions, you first have to get into a mental state of relaxation in order to be receptive for the following affirmation. This sounds more complicated than it really is. It is not necessary to stand on your head for hours or to sit in the lotus position and hum. Instead you should sit down somewhere quiet for a few minutes, close your eyes and do a few breathing and relaxation exercises (the exact explanation of these methods would go far beyond the context of this book and can be found in other suitable books). Once you have relaxed, you should start thinking about your riding. You should do this at the week-end or during the time before you fall asleep, soon after you have woken up, in the bathtub, whenever and wherever you personally are best able to switch off and think of new matters.

OBJECTIVE

You should have long-term as well as short-term objectives: for example, to ride well and correctly over a course at the next show or in the next riding lesson. Long-term you want to be able to ride at a more advanced level. A short-term goal here would be to improve your ability to judge the take-off line, or to practise jumping oxers more frequently, because they cause you particular difficulties. Having a goal is important in order to improve. You need to analyse the state of your riding abilities at all times in order to determine where your deficiencies lie and through which special exercises you can compensate for these defects. If you school on your own, it makes sense to set out a training plan. But even if you have jumping lessons with a trainer, it is necessary to jointly decide how to progress. You need to tell the trainer what you want to achieve. The trainer has a lot of pupils to train and cannot guess the objectives of each individual rider. Often, it is also an incentive for the trainer, if he/she realises through your activity just how serious you are

With the correct mental approach, it is much easier to clear a difficult course.
Photo: Ernst

about your training, he/she will probably be only too glad to help you through special exercises etc. Every now and then you should have a private one-to-one lesson where your specific problems can be treated.

MENTAL TRAINING TO IMPROVE YOUR JUMPING TECHNIQUE

Mental training can also be implemented in a practical manner to improve kinetic processes. As the motion processes are very fast when jumping, it is very difficult to implement corrections or improvements. If you want to improve the position of your lower leg over the fence, for example, you need

If rider and horse are properly prepared, winning a show jumping class will no longer remain a dream. Photo: Hermann

to concentrate very hard to focus specifically on your legs during the jump. In this case, mental training can be used to help. Your subconscious is incapable of differentiating whether you are really sitting on the horse and are training, or whether you are only training in your mind. That is why we experience our dreams at night as being completely real. Mental training has the advantage that your imagination is completely free and without limits and that you can imagine everything as positively as you want to. Do not overdo things, however, with completely unrealistic thoughts that you are suddenly capable of jumping a five-foot-six course in faultless manner. You can supplement your physical training programme through your imagination. Depending on what task you are cur-

rently working on, it is recommended to take ten or fifteen minutes every now and then to think about this specific task. Relax for a certain period of time and then carry out your "dry training"; in other words, imagine how you are sitting on the horse and warming it up for a jumping lesson. Everything must be as realistic as possible, so that you can fool your subconscious. Imagine what clothes you are wearing, how your horse feels and smells, what noises you hear. Including the senses is important to create as realistic an atmosphere as possible. Then start jumping and concentrate on your lower legs: where are they positioned during the jump? Now correct the position of the legs in your mind and feel the legs press against the horse's sides over the imagined jump. In your mind, you can observe yourself and your seat. Then end the session and come back to reality. In your subconscious you have just ridden a jumping lesson in which you learned to keep your lower legs close to the horse's sides during the jump. Your subconscious will now try to realise the lesson you have learned in your next real schooling session.

Mental training is of particular advantage for problems which cannot be solved due to a mental blockage of the rider. If you are experiencing difficulties, for example, in jumping a fence at the correct take-off point, it can help to train for this mentally. In your imagination every jump will be perfect and this helps you raise your self-confidence. You should avoid at all costs allowing negative images to lodge themselves in your mind. Often this is exactly the reason why things go wrong at a fence where you have had a bad feeling all the time. Here, nothing happened except that you imagined that you would fail this fence, and your subconscious has then made sure that it happens in reality. Therefore, you should reject any negative images and delete them from your memory by working on your imagination, so to speak, replacing them with new positive images.

ATTITUDE DURING A COMPETITION

The attitude to and during a competition certainly is one of the most important factors why some sportsmen are always successful and others always have bad luck. People who can imagine how to tackle a task very well and who believe firmly that this is possible, have such self-confidence that it really is easy for them to manage the tasks they are faced with. Others, on the other hand, who are constantly tortured by self-doubt, are held back by their doubts. It isn't for nothing that our successful sportsmen are motivated psychologically before a competition. You should try to develop the same type of positive attitude towards yourself. You are proud of what you have already achieved and are convinced that you can do more, even if it takes time. Unlike other types of sport, riders don't have a direct opponent. Your horse however, which is also influenced by your mental attitude, can feel whether you are in good form and can ride it with trust, or whether you are harbouring fear and doubts, and it will react to your attitude.

Before a show you should take the time and repeatedly imagine how you arrive, how you warm up your horse and then ride the course without a fault. But don't imagine being placed, because a variety of other factors will have an influence on that: for example, your horse, the judges and the other competitors, and these cannot be influenced by your subconscious, unlike the way you ride. If you ride well constantly, success will come in time. Getting placed should not be the one and only reason why you are riding at a show: it is far more important to be satisfied with yourself and your horse and to progress.

The new generation of horse books:
full colour – written by specialists

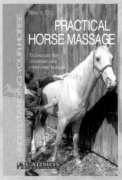

Renate Ettl
Practical Horse Massage

Techniques for loosening
and stretching muscles

96 pages, illustrated
paperback
ISBN 3-86127-903-7
£ 9.95

Ina G. Sommermeier
The Correct Seat

Tips for riders on how
to achieve better balance

32 pages, illustrated
paperback
ISBN 3-86127-933-9
£ 4.95

Anke Rüsbüldt
Mud Fever

Prevention, Diagnosis,
Treatment

32 pages, illustrated
paperback
ISBN 3-86127-935-5
£ 4,95

Anne-Katrin Hagen
First Steps in Dressage

Basic training for
horse and rider

32 pages, illustrated
paperback
ISBN 3-86127-932-0
£ 4.95

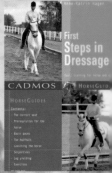

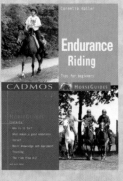

Cornelia Koller
Endurance Riding

Tips for Beginners

32 pages, illustrated
paperback
ISBN 3-86127-930-4
£ 4.95

Anke Rüsbüldt
**Vaccination and Worming
of Horses**

What you need to know

32 pages, illustrated
paperback
ISBN 3-86127-931-2
£ 4.95

Alfons J. Dietz/Daniela Bolze
Long Reining

The Correct Approach

32 pages, illustrated
paperback
ISBN 3-86127-936-3
£ 4.95

Renate Ettl
Western Riding

Tips for Beginners

32 pages, illustrated
paperback
ISBN 3-86127-934-7
£ 4.95

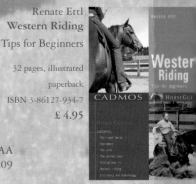

For further informations:
Cadmos/The Editmaster Company
Langham Place · Northampton NN2 6AA
Tel.: 01604-715915 · Fax: 01604-791209
www.cadmos.co.uk

CADMOS
EQUESTRIAN